Straight Talk on Tough Topics

A discussion guidebook for today's
Afrikan-American youth

Chris Jackson

BOYD PUBLICATIONS
NASHVILLE, TENNESSEE

ZondervanPublishingHouse

Grand Rapids, Michigan

A Division of HarperCollinsPublishers

Straight Talk on Tough Topics
Copyright © 1996 by National Baptist Publishing Board

Requests for information should be addressed to:

📖 ZondervanPublishingHouse
Grand Rapids, Michigan 49530

Library of Congress Cataloging-in-Publication Data

Jackson, Chris
    Straight talk on tough topics : a discussion guidebook for today's Afrikan-American
youth / Chris Jackson
       p.   cm.
    Originally published: Nashville : National Baptist Pub. Board, 1994.
    Includes bibliographical references.
    ISBN: 0-310-20819-X (pbk.)
    1. Church work with Afro-American youth. 2. Afro-American youth—Religious
life.   I. Title.
BV4468.2.A34J33   1996
259'.23'08996073—dc 20   96–22617
                                                    CIP

Printed in the United States of America

---

99 00 01 02 03/❖ DH/ 10 9 8 7 6 5 4 3

To my parents and sister who came before me: Mr. and Mrs. Andrew and Christine Jackson and Anita Delaney.

To my brother and sister-in-law who grew up with me: Andrew Leon Jackson II and Rhonda Jean (Bell) Jackson.

To my niece and nephew who are coming after me: Drew and Christi Jackson.

To my wife, and best friend, who has helped me to understand the true meaning of love: Coreen Dawkins Jackson and the Dawkins family.

To my son Joshua Christopher: May the principles promoted in this book become a prominent part of your life as you progress toward becoming a man of God.

CONTENTS

ACKNOWLEDGMENTS

Sincere respect and appreciation is expressed to the following, without whom this book would not have been possible:

The Reverend Kenneth H. Dupree, who formerly served as Director of Publications for the National Baptist Publishing Board and who believed enough in me to make possible the initial publication of this book.

The Reverend Michael Lee Graves, who serves as my pastor at Temple Baptist Church and encouraged me to pursue a literary work.

Dr. John H. Corbitt, who has been a helpful role model for me in his capacity as the National Director of the National Baptist Student Union Retreat and as the Dean of the National Baptist Congress U.S.A., Inc.

God Almighty, who has so lovingly and graciously extended to me abundant life, agape love, and the spiritual gifts to pursue this project.

INTRODUCTION

WHY WE NEED THIS BOOK

Many of today's Afrikan*-American youth are living a painful existence and dying a senseless death. This is primarily because of several social "diseases" that have come to plague the black community. The word "disease" is a combination of a prefix "dis," which "means opposite, absence of, unconnected, or undone"; and the word "ease," which connotes peacefulness, comfort, and proper function. Therefore, to possess a "disease" means that one's normal, peaceful, and proper function has been disconnected resulting in an abnormal, unhealthy separation from one's proper function.

Another term for proper function is "purpose." Bahamian pastor and internationally known speaker, Myles Munroe, has developed a simple, yet tremendously profound, principle concerning purpose.[1] In essence, he states the following: 1) everything in life has purpose; 2) not all purpose is known; 3) where purpose is not known, abuse is inevitable.

---

*Throughout this book, the conventional spelling of the word "Africa" or "African" will be changed to "Afrika" and "Afrikan" for two reasons: 1) there is not a "c" equivalent in most African languages and 2) this spelling with a "k" reflects updated philosophy, thought patterns, and mindsets of the more progressive, independent-thinking and acting Afrikans.

When we are living within our true purposes, we are functionally at "ease," fulfilled, and self-actualized. However, when we are unaware of our true purpose, abuse occurs. The inevitable outcome of perpetual abuse is disease or dis-ease. In order to discover one's true purpose in life, several questions must be asked: Who am I? Why was I created? Who created me? Where have I been? Where am I going? To properly answer these fundamental life questions is to get a firm grip on one's purpose. When we *know* our purpose and *live* our purpose, our very existence becomes an active antidote for "disease."

Every athlete, singer, musician, minister, scientist, writer, and businessperson is most comfortable (at ease) when doing that which he or she was created to do. What were *you* created to do?

Dr. Martin Luther King Jr. was such a great leader simply because that is exactly what he was created to do. Sometimes within the black community, the only existing role models are either negative ones, stereotypical ones, or unrealistic ones. The negative ones are the drug dealers, gang leaders, and exploiters of women. The stereotypical ones are the waiters, clerks, maids, and other blue-collar workers. The unrealistic ones are the professional athletes and top pop singers. (This writer often takes informal verbal surveys of young black boys in an effort to discover their aspirations in life. Almost inevitably in answer to the question "What do you want to be when you grow up?" the answer is "a professional basketball player" or "a professional football player.")

There is nothing wrong with aspiring to be a professional athlete, musician, or even a maid or waiter. The problem arises when one's choices are too limited or too unrealistic to fulfill the vocational purpose for which one was personally created.

Since purpose is being discussed, let us outline the fivefold purpose of this book: 1) to challenge commonly accepted myths and untruths believed *by* black youth and believed *about* black youth; 2) to expose the source of the many current "trouble spots" that exist among today's black youth; 3) to suggest positive and constructive alternatives to popular but dangerous trends and temptations among today's black youth; 4) to encourage young Afrikan-Americans to fulfill their purpose in life and to be all they can be; 5) to provide practical resources for effective ministry with black youth.

The term "youth" is used here to characterize particularly those between the ages of twelve and twenty-two, from junior high to college age. As this book is read, studied, and discussed, do not be afraid to dialogue and even disagree with its points. Raise questions! Suggest another viewpoint! Interact with this material! It is in this way that you will receive the most from the precious time invested in reading this book. May it, in some way, help you, and may you in turn help another.

KILLERS

1

PEER PRESSURE USED

Your companions are like the buttons on an elevator. They will either take you up or they will take you down.

God's Little Instruction Book

ome on! Why not? Everybody will be there! What's wrong with you? Are you scared? Try it just once! You don't know what you're missin'! Please baby, please! Peer pressure. We've all felt it at some point in our lives. Peer pressure can be verbal, as is illustrated above, or it can be applied by our associates' actions alone.

Sometimes peer pressure is intentional, and those around us purposely seek to have us conform to their idea of what should be done. However, other times we are drawn into activities simply due to our *own* deep desire to fit in and to belong. Often this desire for acceptance causes us more problems than when other people deliberately influence us. We all want to be liked by the people who are important to us. This is especially true when there has been a lack of love somewhere in our background. Affirmation and validation by our friends then become substitutes for the love that we truly desire.

As we examine some of the killers of black youth, we will see that peer pressure is a common component that influences many of these killers. This is why it is so important to carefully choose our friends and associates. Question: If you spend 20 percent of your time around positive or spiritual people and 80 percent of your time around negative or non-spiritual people, which of the two groups do you think will influence you most?

The influence exerted by peer pressure appears in many different ways. Consider and discuss the following areas and ways in which our peers influence the way we do things: 1) clothing; 2) hairstyle; 3) speech pattern; 4) amusements; 5) thinking/values; and 6) other areas.

Clothing and hairstyle have always been big issues within the black community. The high value we place on how we look stems partially from our rich Afrikan ancestry. If you went to Afrika today, in each town, large or small, you would inevitably encounter at least two things: a church and a hair-care shop. (Black people all over the world want their 'do to be right!)

Peer pressure's most significant effect, however, is upon our minds. If someone can influence what we think, then they can also influence how we speak and what we do. This has to do with our ultimate values in life and is much deeper than a passing trend. We must be able to differentiate between whether we are simply keeping up with a style, or if peer pressure has taken us to the point of negatively reshaping our values. Question: Will you think, choose, and decide for yourself, or will you allow someone else to do these for you? All of the great people of history have been creative thinkers and innovators. We can never become great by always blending in with our surroundings.

Consider the proverbial analogy between the thermometer and the thermostat. A thermometer reflects the surrounding temperature. If it is hot, the mercury expands and reflects the appropriate temperature. When things get colder, the opposite occurs. But instead of just *reflecting* its surroundings, a thermostat actually *controls* its surroundings! Now, which kind of person are you? A thermometer or thermostat? Your answer to this question will largely determine your success in life and whether you will be a conformist or an innovator.

Usually when discussing peer pressure, we think of others causing us to get into trouble. Question: Is there such a thing as POSITIVE PEER PRESSURE? If so, can you describe it, or have you ever experienced it?

Positive peer pressure also influences others to do things they would not ordinarily do. The difference between negative and positive peer pressure lies in the result of the pressure. If the pressure leads to helping the person to become worse, it's negative. If the pressure leads to helping the person to become *better,* it is positive peer pressure. Of course, one must contend with differing value judgments as to what constitutes better and what constitutes worse. This confusion can be cleared when we apply God's standard rather than a human standard to the situation in question.

Realistically speaking, how should we respond when we are faced with a potentially compromising situation in which negative peer pressure is being used? Here are some suggestions: 1) know in advance what you will and will not do; 2) don't compromise or rationalize; 3) be willing to stand alone if necessary; and 4) love God more than you love your friends.

One popular response to negative peer pressure has been "Just Say No." But how can one just say no to something without having something better to say "yes" to? Christian youth and Christian youth advisors have a responsibility to provide an attractive alternative to the unproductive offering of negative peer pressure. That unsaved young person you are seeking to get involved with your Christian group has every right to ask this question: "If it's wrong for me to go here or to do that, what kind of alternatives are you offering?" In John 10:10, Jesus said "I came that you might have boredom," right? Wrong! He said, "I came that you might have life and life more abundantly." The Christian life lived as God designed is the most vibrant, challenging, and exciting life possible! This fact should give us incentive to encourage others toward a godly direction. This is where positive peer pressure is useful in allowing others to see the joy of a Spirit-filled lifestyle. They will want the Christ in you to be the Christ in them. So what are you waiting for? Pump up the power of the positive peer pressure!

RAP SECTION

1. Discuss some ways you have responded to peer pressure.
2. How do you decide what is right and what is wrong?
3. Does peer pressure have the same effect upon every person in every situation? Discuss.
4. What are some alternatives to the typical negative behavior exhibited by young people in your peer group?
5. Discuss some specific ways in which you could utilize positive peer pressure.

WORD

Read Daniel 1:6–18 and Daniel 3:14–26.
1. In Daniel 1:6–18, Daniel and the three Hebrews requested a separate diet in order to more closely conform to God's will. What is your reaction when you don't want to do something but everyone else is going along? How did Daniel deal with this peer pressure?
2. What was the result of Daniel's decision not to go along with the group? What encouragement does this give to us?

3. King Nebuchadnezzar was upset because the three Hebrews refused to worship the king's god. What are some present day "gods" that you see being worshiped?

4. What do you think about the level of faith and conviction of these three young men? What would you have done? What is significant about the conviction expressed in verse 18 of chapter 3?

5. Are there some things that you absolutely will not do? What are they?

6. How does 1 Corinthians 10:13 relate to the outcome of the situation for the three Hebrews? What consolation does this give us?

2

DRUGS AND ALCOHOL ABUSED

Cocaine and pure grain: Are they really worth the pain?

The man in the commercial holds the egg and says "O.K., last time. This is your brain." As he breaks the egg and drops it into a sizzling hot skillet he says, "This is your brain on drugs. Any questions?"

It is a graphic illustration created to address a graphic problem that has become a modern-day plague in America. Although drug abuse is not limited to any one race, location, or income bracket, it seems that the black community receives a major portion of the backlash and cracklash. This reaction appears in the form of chemical addiction, homicide, fear, and incarceration. Historically, the black man's back has been all too familiar with the latest lash in the land. Isn't it ironic that the drug industry, which is so financially lucrative, would be paid for by those who have little and provides greater financial profit for those who already have much?

Consider the following five major levels of America's drug trade: 1) grower, 2) manufacturer, 3) distributor, 4) seller, and 5) user.

Which two positions do you think gain the most profit from the total transaction? If you selected 2 and 3, you are correct. But when you see TV or newspaper reports of drug arrests, how often do you see instances of drug manufacturers and major distributors who are black? Practically never. Therefore, if somehow the demand for drugs within the community could be significantly curtailed, that would seriously hamper the direct sellers, thus eliminating the major part of the problem.

Before we can talk of curtailing the consumer end of drug abuse, we must first understand the psychology behind the consumption. Following are four major reasons for the abuse of drugs: 1) ignorance as to the purpose of drugs, 2) desire to fit in, 3) attempt to escape from the pain of reality, and 4) curiosity and/or thrill-seeking.

In the first category above concerning purpose, let us test a theory:

Question #1: What is the purpose of drugs?

Response: To cure the ailments of sick people.

Question #2: What happens when well people take drugs?

Response: They become sick.

Abuse, remember, is abnormal use. Our noses were not designed to sniff hallucinogenic white substances, and our veins were not made to transport the extract of an opium poppy plant. When we abuse our body, it makes us pay a high price as a penalty. Sometimes that price is life itself.

"The desire to fit in," the second reason for abuse, has already been somewhat addressed in the first chapter on peer pressure.

Question: Is being accepted by a group worth risking your life with drugs?

The third reason for drug abuse is a deep-seated condition. Some abuse drugs in a vain attempt to escape the pain of reality. Life has become unbearable and suicide is not an option, so the temporary artificial high produced by drugs becomes a convenient escape. However, as usage progresses, that which once provided escape now becomes a trap. Instead of gaining a sense of freedom, the user develops a sense of bondage. Life will never be free of all problems and difficulties. Sometimes those problems can overwhelm even the strongest of us. That is why we need a power greater than ourselves that will not leave us worse than when we started. Such power is found in a personal relationship with Jesus Christ, which will be discussed in a later chapter.

"Curiosity and thrill-seeking" are the fourth dual reasons given for experimenting with drugs. Fulfillment of curiosity is perhaps the most trivial of reasons for drug usage. But trivial or not, there are those who do fall into this category. One would think that as many well-known people who have been devastated by drugs, one's curiosity would have been satisfied by now. Sadly, however, when we fail to learn from the mistakes of others, we are left to the perils of personal experience. Such experiences can, at times, be very harsh teachers.

Time magazine featured an article entitled, "What Would It Take to Get America Off Drugs?" The article stated that the former Bush administration allocated 412 billion dollars to fight drugs but nearly 70% of that went to the "cops and Coast Guard" rather than to preventive education and treatment. The most successful classroom programs use techniques like role-playing to equip self-conscious teens with basic social skills. These skills include "how to conduct a conversation or respond to rudeness, as well as how to resist peer pressure to get high. The working assumption is that youth who can handle their anxiety in social situations are less likely to turn to drugs for comfort." One other startling statistic recorded in the article is that while over three-fourths of the state prison populations in America include drug abusers, no more than 20% receive help while behind bars.[1]

ALCOHOL

Now that we have had a glance at drug abuse, let us turn our attention to alcohol abuse. As we proceed, let us notice that the mere phrase "drug and alcohol abuse" is somewhat redundant.

Question #1: Is alcohol a drug?

Question #2: Is alcohol capable of similar psychological effects as marijuana, for instance?

Question #3: Do the same principles stand regarding alcohol usage as are in effect with other drug usage?

One difference between alcohol usage and other drugs is that, in many states, alcohol consumption suddenly becomes legal to purchase on one's twenty-first birthday. If one is 20 years, 11 months and 29 days old, it is still illegal.

Question #4: Do you detect any hypocrisy in those adults who drink alcohol but cringe at the thought of their children snorting cocaine? While we're on the subject, do you detect any hypocrisy in those adults who profusely puff on cigarettes but recoil at the prospect of their own child smoking marijuana? Like parent, like child.

One common argument in support of those who drink alcohol is that it is okay in moderation. That leads one to ask, what *else* is okay in moderation? Also, who determines the boundaries of moderation?

Question #5: Why do people drink anyway?

Question #6: Is there any value in social drinking?

Question #7: Is there any harm in social drinking?

Question #8: Is there a positive and safe substitute for social drinking?

Question #9: For those Christians who condone "social drinking," is this ever appropriate at a church fellowship function? Why or why not?

As Afrikan-Americans at risk in so many areas, can we ever afford to be even partially out of control? Is even a slight buzz appropriate when each moment of total consciousness is so important? We have a long way to go even with full comprehension, much less with diminished mind power.

Question #10: What is the number one cause overall of teenage death in America?

Answer: Drunk driving.

Question #11: Do you think that drunk drivers started with the intention of drinking in moderation?

Question #12: True or False: About 55% of men and at least 25% of women involved in date rape or acquaintance rape have been drinking or drugging just prior to the attack.

False! Almost 75% of the men and at least 55% of the women had been drinking or drugging just prior to the attack. In an *Entree* magazine article entitled "No Means No," Mark Blice-Baum cites the following:

> An intoxicated man may become more aggressive sexually and less interested in what the woman wants than when he is sober. Alcohol also becomes the excuse he uses to justify his behavior. A woman's perception about what

is happening around her becomes blurred, and her ability to resist an assault is reduced when her verbal and physical abilities are impaired.[2]

Question #13: Is your body really a temple of God?

Question #14: Can you please God while drinking socially?

Question #15: Does drinking hamper your testimony and witness?

Question #16: Can you drink to the glory of God?

"So whether you eat or drink or whatever you do, do it all for the glory of God" (1 Corinthians 10:31). Cocaine and pure grain—are they really worth the pain?

RAP SECTION

Refer to the 16 questions listed throughout this chapter and discuss.

STARTLING STATISTICS

On April 13, 1992, former Surgeon General Antonio Norvello released a report on teenage drinking. Among the findings were the following:

1. Twenty-five percent of eighth graders and 43% of tenth graders were regular drinkers.
2. About one-third of youths committing serious crimes consumed alcohol just before the offense.
3. Over 70% of teen suicides involved frequent use of alcohol or drugs.
4. Alcohol played a part in nearly 40% of drownings and 75% of fatal accidents with all-terrain vehicles.
5. For every injury death, there are 16 hospitalizations and 381 injuries that require medical attention.

An earlier survey released by former Surgeon General Norvello on June 6, 1991, revealed reasons or causes which America's junior and senior high school students say they drink:

1. 40% said they drink when upset;
2. 31% said they drink alone;
3. 25% said they drink when bored; and
4. 25% said they drink to get high.

Many students could not tell the difference between wine coolers, which contain alcohol, and flavored mineral waters, which don't contain alcohol.[3]

WORD

Please read the following verses on the subject of drinking alcohol.
1. Proverbs 20:1—What advice is given here?
2. Daniel 5:1–4—What was the result of Belshazzar's party and how does it relate to youth today?
3. Luke 1:15—What three positive attributes are mentioned concerning John's life and lifestyle? How are they related to each other?
4. Romans 14:21—Besides affecting us, what else could be a result of drinking?
5. 1 Timothy 5:23—What purpose for alcohol is identified here?

3

MONEY
CONFUSED

The love of money is the root of all evil.

1 Timothy 6:10

What is it about money that makes people act so funny? People have been known to argue, fight, and even kill because of money. Some even think that if they only had more money, they would automatically have more happiness. To be sure, a better understanding of how money operates and how to manage it wisely is important. Let us now explore how to develop a healthy appreciation for money without worshiping the dollar.

Principle #1: Nobody owes you anything. Avoid the "somebody owes me" syndrome. As long as we operate with a handout mentally, we will more than likely end up with empty hands. As long as we depend on someone else's generosity for our livelihood, our meals will last only as long as the generous person's charity.

Principle #2: Strive to be debt-free. Many of us live our entire lives cowering beneath the false security blanket of easy credit. We get drawn into the never-ending vacuum tunnel of high interest rates and extended payments. The convenience of credit cards has created a catastrophe in the economic lives of too many people. We are mesmerized by the painless plan of "buy now, pay later." We may go to sleep happy after spending our credit cards to the max, but when the bill arrives, we will find ourselves waking up with a Visa Headache and the Master Card Blues. If you see yourself with this tendency, now is the time for plastic surgery. Cut up those cards and start buying only things for which you can comfortably pay on the front end. There are some credit purchases that are inevitable such as a car or a house. Other than these, use credit as wisely and as rarely as possible.

Principle #3: Learn to pay yourself. Save at least 10% of everything you earn. In addition to tithing 10% of your earnings to God, you should also learn to pay yourself a portion from each paycheck. It is surprising to see how quickly resources accumulate when one is dedicated to a consistent discipline of saving and investing. Inside of most people is a little voice that screams at us each time we get money. That voice goes something like this: "Spend me, spend me!" But if we listen closely enough, there is another voice that softly urges: "Save me, save me!" Those who are building toward a future have listened to the latter voice. Which voice will *you* listen to? It is never too early to begin the healthy habit of saving. Start a coin bank, open a savings account, or purchase a savings bond. But by all means, do something besides spend.

For much too long, Afrikan-Americans have concentrated their efforts toward getting a piece of the pie. It has been noted that a better goal than getting a piece of the pie would be getting a piece of the knife handle. If one has some control of the knife handle, that is what determines how the pie is cut.

We must move more toward being decision makers rather than just decision takers. Financially speaking, this means owning businesses rather than being owned by businesses. It means becoming employers rather than only employees. It means becoming producers rather than primarily consumers. No group of people can ever become economically strong through consuming everything and producing little or nothing.

Question #1: What do black people consume?

Answer: Food, banking services, merchandise at shopping malls, living space, etc.

Question #2: How many black-owned supermarkets, banking institutions, shopping malls, and real estate companies do you know about?

We must begin to produce a generation of black young people who are determined to start producing more now. Don't wait until you are fully grown and established—start now. Look around your communities or school for unmet needs. Once you have identified a need, survey or research the market, identify resources, devise a strategy, then package your product and provide the best service possible.

Three elements that black businesses would do well to include are cleanliness, quickness, and courtesy. Often the absence of these three characteristics is what prevents some black businesses from earning the clientele volume enjoyed by their white counterparts. Remember that if something is worth doing at all, it is worth doing right. Strive for excellence in even the small things in life, and the big things will flow much more easily.

It is understood that not everyone is business-minded and not everyone is destined to be an entrepreneur. However, one thing we can strive to do is at least own our own homes. Since everyone has to live somewhere, we must choose between paying ourselves through mortgage and developing some home equity, or paying someone else for the rest of our lives and never receiving any benefit from a lifetime of rent. The choice is yours, and it is hoped that you will choose wisely.

RAP SECTION

1. Do you ever feel that life owes you something? Why or why not?
2. Have you ever bought anything on credit that you could have bought with cash if you had waited and saved? Why do some of us dislike waiting?
3. Discuss the principle of deferred gratification (forgoing a pleasure today in order to enjoy a greater pleasure tomorrow). How can this be applied to your economic life?
4. Do you currently have a savings plan? If so, is it successful? If not, how could you start one?
5. Share an idea and/or devise a plan for creating your own business.

WORD

Read the parable of the talents (Matthew 25:14–29).
1. What is the basic lesson of this parable?
2. Do the owner's actions seem fair to you? Why? Why not?
3. With which of the three servants do you most closely identify?
4. Do you think it matters to God how you handle your money?
5. How can one's stewardship of money be a reflection of one's relationship and level of commitment to God?

4

HOMICIDE INFUSED

Never choose a permanent solution for a temporary problem.

Question: What is one of the leading causes of death among young Afrikan-American males? Unfortunately everyone knows this chilling answer: Homicide.

More specifically this involves mostly young black folk killing other young black folk—often for no real reason at all. Perhaps the victim looked at the assailant "wrong," ventured into the "wrong" side of town, or wore the "wrong" colors on a T-shirt or a baseball cap. In many communities, very little value is placed upon other people's lives. This is because those who place a low value on others' lives also place a low value upon their own. When people don't care about their own lives or the lives of others, anything can happen. A resident of a notorious government housing area was quoted as saying, "If we could get people to band together more, some of the problems we have would have to move because we would stand and say, 'We don't want this.'" She admitted that even though she had lived in the area for the past twenty-four years she did not feel safe walking in certain areas because "bullets have no eyes and no name."

Perhaps many of the black youths who inhabit the overpopu-
lated and neglected low-income urban areas are just like those
bullets: no eyes (no sight for the future), no name (no feeling of
worth or significance), and, like the bullet, highly explosive.

Question: Why would one black man kill another black man
when there is already so much oppression from sources outside
the black community?

Consider this brief scenario: A man places ten stray cats
inside a 5x5 box. They are fed sparingly and taunted periodically
by the one who put them there. They are not allowed to get out for
exercise and to explore. Yet, through a hole they can see other cats
lounging in luxury and being fed the best of meals. Now, which
of the two groups of cats would you expect to be more likely to
fight each other? Would the cats in the box be primarily to blame
for the incidents of fighting between them?

Many Afrikan-Americans have been categorically locked out of
the American dream. They have been sectioned off and isolated
into an inner-city box that is just an urban version of what has
been done with the American Indians. Many of these black "reservations" are ticking time bombs on the verge of an explosion, such
as the one that occurred in South Central Los Angeles in 1992.

However, regardless of the unhealthy environment in which
some black youth may find themselves, they must rise above their
circumstances. This includes a recognition of the problems and a
coming to grips with the central issues at hand. Yusef Salaam did
face the issue through writing in an *Essence* magazine article entitled
"Men, Macho, and Murder."[1] This Harlem, New York resident is
familiar with death, since he lives in an area where the black
homicide rate is among the highest in the country. "Most of the
murders perpetrated by black men against other black men are
drug-related," he stated. "But Afrikan-American men also kill each
other every day over non-drug-related, pseudo-manhood issues,"

he continued. This open, honest, and up-front article closed with the following statement:

> Today, I try to be more patient with brothers, even if they're wrong and I'm right. And if I'm wrong, I admit that I'm wrong, because it is a double death when one black man winds up in an early grave because of another black man and the black man who sent him there winds up in prison. For in America today prisons have become the new plantations for too many Afrikan-American men.

Prison. Jail. Incarceration. Serving time. Regardless of the description, it still adds up to locked-up potential. Although blacks comprise 12% of America's population, blacks make up 40 to 50% of some prison populations. There is a hidden city full of black men within each city. This unfortunate cycle begins with those who are very young and get caught up in the complex web of juvenile institutions, which include group homes, halfway houses, mental health agencies, probation, and youth detention centers.

Approximately 6.2% of white males aged twenty to twenty-nine are imprisoned or in a release program. But over 23% of Afrikan-American males in the same age group are entangled in the penal system.[2] Several suggestions for handling anger are given in the book entitled, *A Teenager's Guide to Feeling Confident in any Social Situation.*

A sampling of these tips in the author's words are:

1. Anger is a natural emotion. You simply need to control it instead of allowing it to control you. Expressing anger carefully is very important.
2. Before speaking, take a few deep breaths. Feel the tension leave your body. Doing this will help you gain control over your emotions.

3. If you are angered by something someone has done, first ask the person why or how it happened. This is critical because sometimes we misunderstand situations.
4. If the explanation is not satisfactory, don't attack. That will only put your friend on the defensive, making it impossible for him or her to hear you out.
5. Don't just concentrate on your own negative feelings.
6. Never leave the conversation hanging.
7. Saying you're sorry takes a lot of strength.

Afrikan-Americans must learn and practice the discipline of self-control if the expectation is to survive and thrive in the next century and beyond. We all must do our parts in order for the desired result to be achieved.[3]

RAP SECTION

1. Do you know of a young black person who was a victim of homicide? What were the circumstances?
2. How do you usually respond to your own anger?
3. How do you usually respond to someone else's anger?
4. Role play a potentially explosive situation which is defused in a positive way.
5. Is it difficult for you to say you are sorry? Why or why not? Does it take a strong or weak person to apologize?

WORD

Read Luke 6:27–35
1. Is this approach relevant in today's society?
2. Why is it difficult to love your enemies?
3. Have you ever said something nice to someone who had just "gone off" on you?
4. God's way is the opposite of the world's way. Which verses demonstrate this concept to you?

5

RACISM
ACCUSED

Never let someone pull you so low as to hate them.

Martin Luther King Jr.

RACISM (rā-si·zem), as defined by Webster, is the notion that one's own ethnic stock is superior. Prejudice or discrimination is based on racism.[1]

Racism, like Baskin-Robbins, comes in a wide variety of flavors. (Which type have you tasted lately?) Often when considering racism, we focus primarily upon white perpetrators and black victims. Although this is truly the case in the majority of situations, there is plenty of room for variation if we go by the dictionary definition above. Afrikan-Americans are capable of feeling and acting racist toward white people, as well as toward each other. One essential uniqueness of white racism, however, is that the largely white American elite establishment has the power, resources, knowledge, and influence to combine with simple racist feelings and attitudes with power structures and institutionalized systems. This power base has the capability of shutting out anyone who does not fit the often-prescribed criteria for acceptance and full participation in the system. Let us consider racism's types, causes, effects, and cures.

TYPES OF RACISM

Economic Racism

Black Americans comprise 12.1% of the United States' population, yet receive only 7.8% of the country's total personal income. The 1990 median income for black men was $12,868 while white men earned $21,170. Even when educational levels are equal, whites usually earn more than blacks. Consider the following chart:

Median Income for Households in Current Dollars (1993)[2]

Black	$19,533
Hispanic*	22,886
White	32,960
Asian/Pacific Isl.	38,347
All Households Avg.**	31,241

*Persons of Hispanic origin may be of any race.
**Includes other races not shown separately.

This economic disparity between blacks and whites has many reasons. Some of the causes are self-induced and others are a result of some whites getting a head start in the economic race. Often blacks are expected to keep up with the pace and play by the same rules regardless of their starting place. If you have ever seen a 440 track and field athletic race, you will notice that the runner on each successive outside lane has his or her starting blocks placed slightly ahead of the runner on the inside lane. Those who do not understand the reasons behind this placement might cry, "Unfair! Preferential treatment!" However, this differential placement is actually the most fair thing to do since those on the outer lanes have a longer way to run. Afrikan-Americans have made gigantic advancements considering that less than 50 years ago blacks could not even vote in this country, could not eat in the same restaurants with whites, could not reside in the same hotels, could not ride in the front of the bus, and even had separate public bathrooms and water fountains. For young people born after the turbulent 1960s and for any others who have never directly experienced such racism, there is sometimes a tendency to say, "Let's just forget the past and go on toward the future!" Such statements sound wonderful and strike at the center of the ideal. However, life is not always ideal. Much more often life is real, and we must deal with the real because the real will not go away. Let's suppose, for example, that there was a flood or hurricane and a particular city was devastated by the impact. Eventually, the winds would cease and the water would recede. But the stark reality must be faced that even though the initial cause of the damage would have ceased, the effects would still exist. That city could not be expected to rebound overnight. That city could not be expected to progress at the same rate as the town down the road that was unaffected by the disaster. The people who lived through the disaster would not be able to stop remembering the disaster and their loved ones who perished in it. Furthermore, it would be wise of the residents to be on guard or at least to be prepared in the event of another disaster. Let us therefore not be hampered by racism in the past, but at the same time we must remain conscious of the proper steps to take in dealing with current racism and in avoiding racial disaster in the future.

Corporate and Commercial Racism

One indication that racism in America is not over can be found in the national banking system. In 1992, 36% of black applicants for mortgage loans were turned down, while only 16% of white applicants were denied loans. When a Federal Reserve Board in Chicago examined the role of race in the consideration of mortgage loans, it was discovered that marginal minority applicants in their sample were held to higher credit standards than marginal white applicants.[3] *Black Enterprise* reported in 1995 that although the overall rate of bank denial to blacks for home loans was not as high in 1993, this denial rate was still twice as high as the denial rate for whites or Asians.[4]

Some companies seek to soothe their consciences or at least deter criticism by appointing black faces in token places. Sometimes these positions are far from any real decision-making process. However, a word to the wise is that if you do find yourself in a token position, do your very best right where you are because having your foot in the door is better than sitting on the curb outside the door. Better still, create your own door! But we will discuss that in chapter 11.

Legal and Governmental Racism

During the Reagan and Bush eras, racist policies sunk to new lows. Many affirmative action programs initiated by the Carter administration were reversed and funds were taken from social programs and used for military buildup. The Haitian immigrants were unceremoniously returned to their homeland without a hearing. These are all examples of governmental racism.

The legal and penal systems have also been tainted by racism. Minority criminals are sentenced to prison with a much greater percentage of regularity than whites who break the law. The great majority of the crimes committed in the 1990s have been drug-related. Drugs often attract sellers who are jobless and buyers who are hopeless. The black community offers a textbook supply-and-demand scenario for the drug trade.

Educational Racism

The battle against racist educational practices has been a long and difficult one. The reason that this battle is so crucial is because young impressionable minds are at stake, especially during the twelve grade-school years.

Chances are that the typical Afrikan-American high school graduate will have had very little exposure to the greatness and accomplishments of black people. This is because most school textbooks are written from a Eurocentric perspective. Therefore, if black contributions are mentioned, it is done merely in passing or is relegated to some obscure bonus section. But since the United States was built with the backs, blood, sweat, and tears of black people, their many accomplishments in each strata of society should be intricately woven within the fabric of this great tapestry called America.

Another crucial factor in the educational process is the inaccurate judgment of some academic placement workers and vocational guidance personnel. Black youth are disproportionately labeled as slow learners when in reality, they may simply be "different learners." Students who are hyperactive, chronically irritable, or who have short attention spans, need not be automatically put into special education classes. More time, testing, and tenderness must be put into the process before a youth is categorized. This labeling tends to lower the aim of some black students rather than encouraging them to discover their fullest potential. Countless would-be doctors, lawyers, and bank presidents have instead become much less, chiefly because a so-called counselor discouraged them rather than encouraged them.

Religious Racism

Since some people are racist and churches are made up of people, it is understandable that some churches would reflect the racism of their members. Racism is deeply ingrained and sometimes seems to stubbornly persist even in close proximity to the truth of God. Eleven o'clock on Sunday mornings continues to be the most racially segregated period of the week in American society.

But blacks and whites worshiping separately has more to do with style than with racism. Religious racism on college campuses can be observed in the often subconscious paternalistic attitudes of some white campus groups. Some well-meaning whites are quick to say, "Come on over and join us," without also mentioning that to "join us" also means to "become like us" if you are to fit in. Campus groups such as Baptist Student Union have made serious and significant advances in ministry *with* blacks rather than just ministering *to* blacks.

Psychosocial Racism

A great deal of the racism experienced by black youths is psychosocial and very subtle. It can easily go undetected by the insensitive eye and ear. In his book, *Black Men: Obsolete, Single, Dangerous?*[4] Haki Madhubuti lists five daily battles most black people fight. According to him, these battles include color, poverty, hair, fear, and language.[5] At least a couple of these battles deserve additional examination. Color has long been a tender topic both inside as well as outside the black community. In the 90s we are enjoying a powerful resurgence of appreciation for our beauty, culture, and Afrikan heritage. Even the white society seems to be relaxing its formerly narrow interpretation of feminine beauty as white-skinned, blonde, straight-haired, blue-eyed, slim-framed, straight-nosed, and thin-lipped. There have been three Afrikan-American "Miss America" winners and finalists as well as several top black professional models. The beauty industry standards now are actually moving more toward darker complexions, wider lips, and fuller frames.

It is encouraging to see that some things are changing, although it seems that other subtle racial concepts will be with us forever. Many of the racist notions which are difficult to shake are built into the language. For example, consider the following list of good and bad images:

EUROPEAN CONCEPT

Positive/Good/Pure	*Negative/Bad/Evil*
white hats	black hats
white horse	black horses
white lies	black lies
white heart	black heart
angel's food cake	devil's food cake

Other negative black phrases include black list, black ball, black market, and black sin. Negative black imagery is everywhere. Have you noticed that when crimes such as robbery or rape are reported in the newspaper, a black suspect's color is usually highlighted either in print or by a prominent photo? Newspapers tend not to play up the color angle as much when the suspect happens to be white. This is precisely why there is a need for more responsible black newspaper writers, TV anchors, and magazine editors. Blacks need to have more input into how blacks are interpreted and presented to the public.

Black Racism

Black racism comes in at least two forms: intra-black racism and hyper-black racism. Intra-black racism deals with the misguided concept that just because another black individual has some other minute difference, this person is seen as a threat or as an enemy. These "differences" could be as insignificant as skin shade, area of residence, or peer group. Although not identical in nature, it is easy to see that some black racism is based upon many of the same principles as white racism.

What is called here "hyper-black racism" is an attitude that is so preoccupied with "fighting the white man" that the person is blinded to the fact that not all whites are necessarily "bad" and not all blacks are necessarily "good." Hyper-black racism supports an ultra-separatist perspective, which often casts a negative light on anything and anyone who happens to not be black.

CAUSES OF RACISM

History and Tradition

The roots of racism go deep into the soil of American history. It is impossible to properly understand America's current racial scene without also understanding America's racial history. Africa was pilfered and dissected by merciless marauders from Europe. This trend continued as conscienceless Spaniards expanded into the Caribbean and exterminated the gentle Arawack people who were the original inhabitants of Jamaica. Still greedy for power, they sailed north and landed in America. America was already inhabited by natives, but since these new visitors wanted the land, the natives, incorrectly called *Indians* by Columbus, were continuously pushed west to Indian reservations.

As the Europeans began to work the land especially in the south, they discovered that cotton would grow well there. It was a good cash crop since everyone needed clothing. But because cheap labor was hard to find, someone came up with an evil idea: transcontinental slavery. So the ships sailed and Afrikans were purchased from other Afrikans. Those who survived the incredibly cruel Middle Passage were separated from their families, stripped of their language, clothes, their culture, and sold like animals on auction blocks throughout the South to the highest bidder. They were treated as property and forced into free labor for 300 years.

Eventually America's Civil War erupted, largely over slavery. The anti-slavery north was victorious. Lincoln issued the Emancipation Proclamation banning slavery, and former slaves were promised 40 acres and a mule. Of course, that promise was never fulfilled. There were several decades of ridiculous Jim Crow laws that restricted Negro rights and privileges. Finally, one day a little seamstress from Alabama decided, on that particular day in Montgomery, not to move from her seat on the bus but to stay seated because of her conviction of what was right, not to give a white man her bus seat. She was arrested and sent to jail for such insubordinate behavior. This mild-mannered seamstress named Mrs. Rosa Parks was a faithful church member. Her pastor, the Rev. Ralph David Abernathy, was a very close friend of Dr. Martin Luther King, Jr., and they met to devise a plan of action to address Mrs. Parks' arrest. Thus, the Montgomery Improvement Association was born. This led to the Montgomery Bus Boycott, which ignited the Civil Rights struggle. The rest is still history in the making. It should be easy to see that the bus boycott, which occurred in 1955-1956, was not very long ago. Many of the perpetrators and victims of racism are still alive.

Wendell Dawson summarizes this perpetuation of the past in the following statement:

> In order to maintain a system where human beings would be held as farm animals, it was necessary to dehumanize the African. This made it possible for the slave owner to rationalize his brutality to the African. The dehumanization process resulted in extensive psychic damage to the African which has continued to the generation which exists today. Black people began internalizing these messages and grew to hate themselves and others in the group. This self-hatred prevents the African-American from respecting himself and respecting the accomplishments of other African-Americans.[6]

Economic Advantages — We have already observed that haves will never voluntarily share their substance with the have-nots. Since most of the haves in America are white and most of the have-nots are black, there is a built-in system of separation that exists.

Selfishness and Greed — Greed is characterized by a continuous craving for the overabundant. Greed says, "The more I have, the more I want." Greed is always unwilling to share. Therefore, when greed meets need, the occasion is not very harmonious.

Power, Ego, Control — Some people have an inherent desire for domination and a constant craving for control. This scene is feverishly demonstrated each working day on the floors of the New York Stock Exchange and in other places. Ego won't let go until it is in total control of everyone and everything.

Fear, Ignorance, Unfamiliarity — This category is one of the strongest perpetrators of racism. There is always a sense of fear connected with the unfamiliar. We naturally fear the unknown.

It is hard to say why people would rather concentrate on the differences between them rather than on the similarities. *Essence* carried an article in which five white men of various ages were interviewed and one commented about why white men fear black men:

> I'm going to come off [sounding] like a Farrakhanite here but I think the white man is a far more fearsome figure in history than the black man. This is a way of shifting the guilt from him and his role in America. I also think it's about a sexual fear, or sexual competition. It has to do with slavery essentially. Black women were chattel and white men could have their way with them. The black man was kind of aced out of the picture, but to the extent that he was even considered, he was demonized. And so you get the notion of a superpotent black man.[7]

Sin — When racism in any form is reduced to its lowest common denominator, the bottom-line cause is SIN. Sin is defined as unconformity to God's will and missing God's mark. Since God made everyone, God is not pleased when one part of His creation feels or acts unfavorably toward another aspect of His creation. God is the very essence of love. The opposite of love is hate, so when we hate a brother or sister, we are living in opposition to God.

CURES FOR RACISM

Love/Forgiveness

Truth can be restored to the blindness of racism by the light of love. Humanly speaking, it is most difficult to love someone who hates you, but love is a force which supercedes the power of hate. Consider the following wise observations on the nature of human relations from *Apples of Gold*: "Never let a man pull you so low as to hate him." "The only safe way to destroy an enemy is to make him your friend." "Love is not soft like water, it is hard like a rock, on which the waves of hatred beat in vain." "To understand is to pardon." "Love your enemies." "Hate is a prolonged manner of suicide."[8]

The January 1996 issue of *Ebony* magazine provided a powerful quotation by the Reverend Dr. Martin Luther King Jr. on this timely topic of love:

I am convinced that love is the most durable power in the world. It is not an expression of impractical idealism, but of practical realism. Far from being the pious injunction of a Utopian dreamer, love is an absolute necessity for the survival of our civilization. To return hate for hate does nothing but intensify the existence of evil in the universe. Someone must have sense enough and religion enough to cut off the chain of hate and evil, and this can only be done through love. Moreover, love is creative and redemptive. Love builds up and unites; hate tears down and destroys. The aftermath of the "fight fire with fire" method ... is bitterness and chaos, the aftermath of the love method is reconciliation and the creation of the beloved community … Yes, love—which means understanding, creative, redemptive goodwill, even for one's enemies—is the solution to the race problem.[9]

Integration vs. Esteem

It was once thought by blacks and whites alike that integration was the single answer to the race problems in America. They were wrong. Integration was tried but the predictable happened. Anytime a small and *less* powerful group is merged with a larger *more* powerful group, the larger group is merely enlarged, but the smaller group is often absorbed. In essence, American integration asked for a bad trade: a white ideological increase in exchange for a black cultural decrease. Wendell Dawson, quoted earlier in this chapter, believes that before integration can even begin to be considered, Afrikan-Americans must first engage in some inner healing, self-love, and group love. "We are probably in need of some collective cathartic experience whereby we can exorcise the demons of inferiority and self-hatred which have prevented us from working and living together as other ethnics do," he states. He concludes that integration can only become feasible when there is "complete and total honor and respect for the African-American(s) as well as for [their] culture and history."[10]

Appreciation of Diversity

If America is to survive and thrive she must learn to respect and relish her rich, culturally diverse population. This is the unique strength of America. The U.S.A. is not all colors blended together with no distinction. Rather, it is many different colors coexisting side by side with distinct beginnings and ends, but arranged together in such a way to create a thing of great beauty.

Equity

According to Joseph Lowery, president of the Atlanta-based Southern Christian Leadership Conference, blacks in America are in need of EQUITY, not equality. "Equity" is defined as the quality, state, or ideal of being just, fair, and impartial. Speaking at a Minority Business Opportunity Fair, Lowery stated that blacks have generally achieved equality, but lack equity.

Lowery explained the difference between the two by telling a story about a man who initially advertised that he was producing rabbit-meat sausage. However, he began to use horse meat whenever he ran out of rabbits. When inspectors questioned the man about his improper use of horse meat rather than rabbit meat, the man said that the two meats were "equal." He said, "every time I put in one rabbit, I put in one horse!" Equality? Yes! Equity? No!

In explaining the value and wisdom of the concept of preferential treatment, Lowery further stated: "Don't be scared by preferential treatment. You've got five fingers and if one of them is cut, bruised and bleeding, let me strongly suggest that you give one of them preferential treatment. Not for the sake of the lone finger, but for the sake of the whole hand."[11]

Maturity/Responsibility

One of the principles of the Afrikan-American Cultural Celebration of Kwanza is "Kujichagulia" which means "self-determination." Afrikan-Americans cannot continue to look to any other group of people for assistance in determining destiny. This is a valuable and powerful resource which must be tapped from within. The time has come when the notion of someone "owing us" cannot be depended upon. Following the first Million Man March, there was a flurry of strong feelings on the part many Afrikan-American men, and in several cases there was positive and practical channeling of this tremendous energy, which resulted from the nation-wide black male wake-up call. However, upon attending one of the follow-up meetings on a particular college campus, this writer was struck by the excessive amount of "white-folk-blaming" which seemed to have occupied a major segment of the total time spent in the meeting. If Afrikan-Americans continually define themselves in terms of what someone else has or has not done, they will forever be doomed to view the whole of life through the myopic channel of "us and them." It is high time to wake up and realize that the world is so much larger than black and white issues in America. The key is not to ignore or disregard the issue, because it obviously is an important one as was seen in the aftermath of the O. J. Simpson verdict. However, we must not allow the issue to so totally possess us to the point of disabling our ability to function beyond bitter verbal attacks against Europeans and pseudointellectual displays of philosophizing about the race problem without any concrete solutions for solving it.

In his refreshingly practical and straightforward book, *Beyond Blame*, Michael A. Grant in chapter 6 issues "An Honest Challenge to Black America: Grow Up." This seems like such a shocking statement because few people have dared to say such a thing in print before. Few people like to be told to grow up, but when it is sincerely said, it is said for the good of the other person. Grant explains his position in this way: "Like it or not, black America has come of age. We are now adults. As adults, we must become more responsible about our survival in this country. We must assume a lion's share of the responsibility for our individual and communal survival. We can no longer spend our money on *what we want* and then expect whites to provide our languishing communities with *what they need*."[12]

Conclusion

In conclusion, let us consider ten simple yet practical steps for enhanced cultural relations in everyday life. These principles could forever change your life.

1. Be yourself
2. Relate to individuals, not groups
3. Celebrate differences
4. Share our oneness
5. Seek the best in others
6. Take the initiative for racial improvement
7. Keep communication open
8. Respect everyone
9. Let God lead
10. Don't ever give up

RAP SECTION

1. Discuss the causes of racism listed in this chapter. Do you agree with them? Some of them? All of them? Would you add other causes?
2. Do you feel that racism has had any effect upon you? If so, describe the effect. If not, why not?
3. Discuss each of the ten practical steps listed at the conclusion of this chapter. A) Have any of these suggestions ever worked for you? Explain. B) Give examples of each of the steps. C) Can you think of other steps?

ROLE PLAY

Role play the following situations:

1. You are in a group of friends and one person in the conversion makes a harsh and untrue racist remark about a particular race or ethnic group other than your own. Do you say or do anything? If so, what? If not, why not?

2. You are personally insulted verbally by a racist remark or implication. How do you handle it?
3. You are working on a job in which your co-workers give you the cold shoulder and do not include you in many conversations or plans. How do you respond?

WORD

1. Read Colossians 3:11 and discuss how it relates to current race relations.
2. Continue in this chapter with verses 12–17. Pick out specific aspects of this passage that would be helpful in race relations.
3. Read Luke 4:18–19. This is the Scripture selected by Jesus during His first recorded reading in the temple. Do you see any connection between this Scripture and black people all over the world? Elaborate upon the specifics.
4. Jesus was forever getting into "trouble" with the Jewish establishment for His conversation with and about those Gentiles who were considered racial and social outcasts. Review the examples below and discuss specific ways you feel Jesus would have reacted to current comparable social situations.
   a. John 4:7–30 —What were the different relationship barriers faced by Jesus in seeking to relate to this woman?
   b. Luke 10:29–37—How does Jesus define a neighbor? How do you define a neighbor?

6

SEX
MISUSED

Sex without commitment is a cheap substitute for intimacy.

SEX AND THE MEDIA

We are living in a society saturated with sex. Almost everywhere one turns, there is something or someone selling or suggesting the subject of sex. Foremost among those communicators of carnality is television. The major information source for the majority of Americans, according to a 1990 Neilson study, is the television. Network decision makers are primarily concerned with one thing: MONEY! Revenue is based on ratings, and sex sells.

The television industry offers the following major types of programming formats: comedies, soap operas, talk shows, feature movies, entertainment reviews, information shows, music videos, and news. In the various categories listed above, sex is prominently featured in practically all of them. Test this by thinking of an example from each of these categories. During the heyday of "The Cosby Show," the black family was finally portrayed in a positive, wholesome, professional manner. That show did a great deal to constructively alter many incorrect perceptions of the black family and to model healthy black sexuality within a marriage. Unfortunately, there were not enough shows like it to effectively counteract all the harsh "in your face" kind of "I-gotta-have it-give-it-to-me-baby-I-wancha-body-right-now" images projected by such programs as MTV and BET Video Soul.

Just as the misguided message of immediate sex-on-impulse is emphasized on television, it also makes a tremendous impact through the radio. Have you actually listened to the lyrics of songs lately? Let's take another little survey: Name ten currently popular secular songs. How many deal directly with making love or some message about sex?

Recorded music is a very popular black medium. Gradually, since the late 1960s and early 1970s, recorded music has become increasingly bold in the area of sexually explicit lyrics. Consider the following degenerative progression since the 1960s:

1960s	The Isley Brothers	"It's Your Thang"
1970s	Marvin Gaye	"Sexual Healing"
1980s	George Michael	"I Want Your Sex"
	Prince	(Too numerous to list)
	Salt N Pepa	"Push It "
1990s	Shabba Ranks	"X-tra Naked"; "Slow and Sexy"
	Adina Howard Solo	"Freak Like Me"; "Where Do You Want Me To Put It"

The above songs are still quite soft in comparison to some of the material being recorded by some of the current rap groups.

Question: How many top-ten song lyrics can you quote from memory? Do you feel that the music has any effect on you?

We are all collections of our total life experiences and influences. Almost every image and sensation to which we are exposed has a conscious or unconscious effect on us. The more graphic the lyrics and the more repetitious the message, the greater the impact and the more lasting the impression. Just as dirty water must be filtered before being consumed, so must your music and movies be filtered before you allow them into your system.

THE TEEN SEX SCENE:
WHO'S HAVING SEX, AT WHAT AGE, AND WHERE?

In 1990, the Centers for Disease Control conducted a national survey to determine sexual behavior among high school students. The results indicated that over half of the nation's high schoolers have had sex. The percentage of sexually active students climbed from 40% of the ninth graders to 48% in tenth grade, 57% in eleventh and 72% in twelfth grade.[1] College students were not included in this particular survey. However, it is a fact that most college students are away from immediate parental oversight, have access to more privacy, and are in frequent proximity to many others of the opposite sex. These factors alone substantiate the estimate that upwards of 90% of college students probably have engaged in sex at least once.

The results of the above survey, reported in 1992, showed that high school males were more likely to have been sexually active than girls (61% to 48%). Racially speaking, 52% of white students, 53% of Hispanic students, and 72% of black students were reported to have been sexually active according to the survey.

The following is an edited transcript of a conversation between a newspaper reporter and three teenage counselors for a youth crisis pregnancy center.

Reporter: How sexually active are students in your schools?

Nate: Very, I mean it's like an everyday basis. As soon as you get out of school, somebody goes to somebody's house.

Reporter: What percentage of high school students would you estimate are sexually active?

Nate: I would go far enough to say at least seven out of ten.

Kena: In my high school, it seems like as soon as people start hitting high school, you know, eighth grade, it's just like they're all gone.

Reporter: How about before that?

Nate: In junior high, you do have some who are sexually active. I would say in junior high, less than half. High school is a seriously big change. You see a lot of girls that come to school every day with a second set of skin on. Tight clothes.

Kena: Teens think they're free. And get wild.

Nate: It's a statement: I'm in high school—I'm almost grown —I can live like I want to live.

Kena: Freshmen need to go through just as rigorous a course of sex education. This health stuff is not getting the job done. We still have teen pregnancy. It has dropped, but it is still there.

Reporter: When and where are kids having sex?

Davise: When their parents aren't home.

Nate: In the park. Behind the bleachers. In the gym. In the band room. They feel like nobody is going to peep around the corners and catch them. So hey, let's go for it. This is not just when everybody has gone to the cafeteria. This is like (under the bleachers) during pep rallies. In the bathroom. Lock the door so nobody would get in ... Things like that. They just go. They just go.[2]

MALE/FEMALE DIFFERENCES

Even though we know of some of the obvious differences in men and women, the more subtle differences often escape us. For instance, men are primarily stimulated by sight while most women are primarily stimulated by emotions. A trip to the super-market reveals that the reading material produced for men emphasizes photographs of women. Female-oriented reading material, however, emphasizes the emotional aspect of relation-ships through romance novels.

Although there are many opinions about the use of birth control, the major types are here along with their costs and rates of effectiveness.

Method	Effectiveness	Cost
Foams, Creams, Jellies, Capsules, Sponges	79%	$3-$8
Rhythm Method	80% (typical use)	$5-$8 & up
Diaphragm & Cervical Cap	82% (typical use)	$50-$85
Condom	88%	$3-$8 box
Intrauterine Device	97% (typical use)	$150-$300
The Pill	97% (typical use)	$40-$90 w/exam
Sterilization	99%	(varies but expensive)
Norplant	99%	$500-$600
Abstinence	100%	$0

As you examine this list, which of the methods above would you say is the best choice financially, functionally, psychologically, and spiritually? Much as been said concerning safe sex and so-called "safer sex." However, even this term is somewhat troubling, especially in this day of rampant sexually transmitted diseases. If you were getting ready to sky dive and were offered a "safer" parachute, how would you react?

COMMON RATIONALIZATIONS
FOR CHOOSING PREMARITAL SEX

What are the reasons young people typically give for participating in premarital sex? An informative booklet entitled, *Making Decisions About Sex, Drugs and Your Health*,[4] lists the following chart:

Why Some Girls Have Sex

"He loves me. If I get pregnant, we'll get married and have a great life together."

"Having sex will make us closer. He'll love me more and we'll talk more."

"I'll be more popular if I stop being so old-fashioned and give in sometimes."

What Really Happens

"We got married and had the baby but we fought so much, we broke up."

"Since we started having sex we don't talk or just have fun the way we used to."

"I wish I'd waited for someone special. The wrong kind of guys are asking me out."

Why Some Guys Have Sex

"If I don't push her to have sex, she'll think I don't really like her or I'm gay."

"It feels great, and besides, I'd know if she had one of those diseases."

"I'm not that great at sports, and I'm kinda short for my age. Me, a father? Ha."

What Really Happens

"I really liked her a lot, but she broke up with me because I kept pushing her for sex."

"I never guessed she had (a disease). I guess you can't always tell."

"Last year I got a girl pregnant. I never thought it would happen to me."

Have you ever encountered any of the above situations? If not, how about the following attempts at persuading one's partner into sex?

1. *The Fit-In Technique:* "Everybody else is doing it."
2. *The Pity Technique:* "It's too late now, baby; I can't help myself!"
3. *The Prove-It Technique:* "If you really love me, you would let me."
4. *The Compromise Technique:* "O.K., just this once and I won't ever ask you again."
5. *The Guilty Technique:* "I can't believe you could lead me up to this point and then stop now."
6. *The Same-Boat Technique:* "Aw, you know you want me just as bad as I want you."
7. *The Heart-Melting Sensitive Male Rap Technique:* "Darling, my feelings for you have grown so strong and deep that sometimes I think about you and wonder how I could be so lucky to have such a beautiful, sweet, and caring lady like you. Please allow me to express to you in this way just how very much I do love you."
8. *The Ultimate Old-Fashioned, No-Shame-Break-Down-and-Beg-Technique:* "Baby please, please, pleeeeeeeeease!!!"

The above is just a small general sampling of stock lines that have been successfully used for years to persuade weak-minded individuals to share their bodies with someone who loves himself infinitely more than he loves the other person. Of course, there are hundreds of other lines being created and tried out every night and day. Those who are experts at this line game realize that if one line does not work, they just keep trying and eventually they will come up with the right combination. Before these con artists are discovered, they have entered the safe, stolen the goods, and moved on to the next challenge. For some, the challenge of a particular sexual partner becomes a game. The thrill is in the pursuit, and when the object of the pursuit is captured, it is then on to bigger and better things.

Question: What is your most important sexual organ?

Answer: Your mind!

FOUR MINDSETS

Please respond to the following questions based on what you personally believe is right. Base your response upon the personal standards and practices by which you currently live. When it comes to sex between males and females, under which of the following conditions would you say that sex is appropriate and advisable?

	Check One	
	Yes	No
1. Sex is O.K. if both partners truly love each other.	☐	☐
2. Sex is O.K. if both partners are mature enough to be responsible for their actions.	☐	☐
3. Sex is O.K. only within the context of a godly marriage.	☐	☐
4. I'm just not sure exactly when sex is O.K.	☐	☐

Please take a few minutes now before reading further. Decide which category most accurately describes your lifestyle and mindset. Now, let us interpret each of the mindsets.

If you selected #1, you probably have a natural mind. Natural-minded individuals comprise the most common category of people. Those with a natural mind have been untouched by anything higher than the natural human tendencies with which they were born. This type of mind is described in 1 Corinthians 2:14: "But a natural man does not accept the things of the Spirit of God; for they are foolishness to him, and he cannot understand them, because they are spiritually appraised" (New American Standard Bible).

The second category is an interesting one. If you selected this one, you probably have a canine mind. Young puppies have no strong sexual drive but as they mature, instinct takes over and they are driven by their hormones. First Corinthians 6:12–13 and 18–20 puts it this way:

> I may do anything, but that does not mean that every-thing is good for me. I may do everything, but I must not be a slave to anything. Food was meant for the stomach and the stomach for food; but God has no permanent purpose for either. But you cannot say our physical body was made for sexual promiscuity; it was made for the Lord, and in the Lord is the answer to its needs. … Avoid sexual looseness like the plague! Every other sin that a man commits is done outside his own body. Have you forgotten that your body is the temple of the Holy Spirit, who lives in you and is God's gift to you, and that you are not the owner of your own body? You have been bought and at a price! Therefore bring glory to God in your body (Phillips Modern English Bible).

Now, let us continue to the next category in our list of mind-sets. If you selected #3, you have selected the choice of the divine mind. The divine-minded person views all of life from the divine, or godly perspective. God's Word encourages us to "Let this mind be in you, which was also in Christ Jesus" (Philippians 2:5, King James). Here is the divine mind on the subject of marriage and sex: "Marriage is honorable and faithfulness should be respected by you all. God himself will judge those who traffic in the bodies of others or defile the relationship of marriage" (Hebrews 13:4, Phillips).

Category 4 is for those with a double mind. Double-minded people usually have a difficult time deciding on one thing because they believe a little of this and a little of that. James 1:8 (King James) says, "A double-minded man is unstable in all his ways."

Since we are what we think, it is very important to possess the right mindset, especially with regard to something as important as sex.

CHOICES

No matter how much you hear from parents, preachers, or peers regarding sex, it is ultimately up to YOU to decide how you will personally deal with this area. Whatever you decide will positively or negatively affect almost every other area of your life. Let us consider the advantages and disadvantages of premarital sex from a youth perspective. In his book, *A Students' Survival Manual,*[5] Alan N. Schoonmaker lists the following disadvantages of abstaining from premarital sex (Of, course this is from a natural or worldly point of view):

1. Premarital sex helps you develop your own moral code and make your own decisions.
2. If it is your partner's first time, he or she may feel more warm and special toward you.
3. If your partner drops you after having sex, you will know the person was not sincere.

At this point, we must supply some additional so-called advantages of premarital sex from a worldly perspective.

4. Allows girls to instantly increase in campus popularity and to easily attract dates.
5. Provides guys a sense of status and pride.
6. Allows you to test drive your partner. Provides some of the benefits of marriage without the commitment.

If some of the above advantages seem humorous, shallow, unrealistic, or even silly, it is probably because you are viewing these so-called advantages from a different perspective than the natural. In all fairness to Alan Schoonmaker, his book also provides a substantial case in support of abstaining from premarital sex. His reasons include the following:

Advantages of Abstinence

1. Premarital sex can produce guilt and lower your self-respect.
2. Premarital sex can lower respect from other people (including your partner).
3. Premarital sex can decrease your chances for marriage. (Some people shun "used goods" when it comes to a permanent commitment.)
4. Premarital sex rarely determines partner compatibility.

As with the first list, please allow us to add some other significant advantages to this list.

5. Abstinence keeps sex from distracting the couple's attention from more important aspects of the relationship such as trust, communication, unselfishness, honesty, etc.
6. Abstinence helps increase respect between partners and helps to avoid the challenge-conquer-exit syndrome.
7. Helps avoid future guilt feelings, flashbacks, and sexual comparisons.
8. Helps avoid unwanted pregnancies, abortions, and unwed parenthood.
9. Severely decreases the possibility of contracting sexually-transmitted diseases.
10. Abstinence from premarital sex is a form of personal discipline as well as obedience to God.

TWO QUICK ANALOGIES

1. Sex inside a godly marriage is like putting money in your bank. It increases your assets, raises the interest level, and gives you greater returns. Sex outside of marriage is like taking money from someone else's bank.
2. Sex inside a godly marriage is like putting motor oil inside your engine. It cuts down on friction and helps things turn more smoothly. Sex outside a godly marriage is like pouring motor oil on the outside of the engine. This causes the engine to smoke and severely cuts down on driver visibility.

FOUR CASUALTIES OF PREMARITAL SEX

In our consideration of sexuality among black youth, we must briefly devote some attention to four particularly devastating issues related to this topic.

Teen Pregnancy

The number of teen pregnancies within the Black community is tremendously high. The Children's Defense Fund (CDF) reports that in 1991, thirty-eight states reported that over 18% of births to black women were to teenagers. A more recent CDF report contends that while overall teen birth rates dropped somewhat in 1993, a growing number of total teen births take place outside of marriage. The CDC offers this quick glance at *one day in the life of black children in America.*[6]

Everyday …
1,334 black teens become sexually active
1,257 black babies are born to unmarried mothers
  907 black teenagers get pregnant
  420 black teenagers give birth
  375 black teenagers have abortions

367 black teenagers drop out of school

245 black babies are born at low birth weight (under 5.5 lbs.)

33 black babies die before their first birthday

1 black young adult under 25 dies from HIV infection

These are more than numbers, because each statistic points to yet another family without both parents. In God's marvelous wisdom, he designed us so that bringing a child into the world would be impossible without the cooperation of a man and a woman. This collaboration was not by mistake. Let us never lose sight of the need for the unique and loving influence of both parents in the development of a child.

Abortion

Where there is unwed pregnancy and teen pregnancy, there is also abortion. The Centers for Disease Control reported that in 1989 that for every 1,000 live births to teens under age fifteen, 900 others had abortions. In 1974, girls under 15 had about 1,200 abortions for every 1,000 live births. With all ages combined, there were 1.4 million abortions in 1989, which is up from 1.3 million in 1980. Overall, 80% of all abortions are performed on unmarried women.[7]

Sexually Transmitted Disease

Another by-product of premarital sex is sexually transmitted disease (STD). Although blacks comprise roughly 12% of the U.S. population, the Centers for Disease Control and Prevention report that of the 13-year-old and older males diagnosed with AIDS, 30.2% are black men. Of the total U.S. women diagnosed, a soaring 57.0% are black women. Of the total U.S. children diagnosed with AIDS, sadly 59.1% are black children. The STD least-wanted list includes the following pain-producing and life-taking infections:

Condition	Can Lead To
Genital Herpes (the most common STD)	nervous system damage
Chlamydia	pelvic inflammatory disease, female sterility, inflammation of the testes
Gonorrhea	genital and anal discharge, and pain
Syphilis	brain damage/paralysis

HIV/AIDS

AIDS (Acquired Immune Deficiency Syndrome) is the most feared of all STDs because of the savage and merciless manner in which it ravages its victims. There is a seriously disproportionate number of AIDS cases in the Afrikan-American community. Although blacks comprise 12% of the U.S. population, reported AIDS cases as of October, 1992 were over 30% black.[8]

AIDS is the full-blown condition of people who have become sick from HIV (Human Immunodeficiency Virus). HIV is the condition which immediately precedes AIDS. It can take 5 to 10 years for HIV to become AIDS. In one particular U.S. state investigated for this book, black AIDS cases were 28.2% of the total statewide, but HIV cases were 53.5%! Since HIV takes a while to develop, what can we expect within the black community in 5 to 10 years? AIDS is not prejudiced. It is an equal opportunity disease. Chances are that you know at least one person who had AIDS and has died with the disease. If you thought it was only a disease for gays or drug addicts, please give Magic Johnson a call. Or better yet, call the National AIDS Hotline at 1-800-325-AIDS. This is a toll-free call and they are also the information source for the AIDS information included in this section.

ABSTINENCE

A few weeks after Magic Johnson announced that he was HIV-positive, he told the Lansing State Journal that he would urge unmarried people to abstain from sex rather than practice safer sex. "Right now, I want to gear to young people that the best sex is no sex," he said. But is celibacy a viable option these days? Abstinence is becoming an increasingly popular option in this fear-stricken decade. A new concept that has surfaced is "second virginity." This is one of the terms used by P.A.C.T. (Parents and Children Together). PACT urges young people to give virginity a second chance. "I've had students tell me that they didn't know they had a choice [not to have sex]," said Jeanne Wacks-Walker, a PACT founder. "You have a choice to start, a choice not to start, and a choice to stop." The way PACT works is the sexually-active student decides to abstain for a period of time determined by the student. A personal commitment statement is then signed by the participant and ongoing support is provided. There are those who may say that abstinence is unrealistic. To them Walker says that "abstinence is as real as AIDS in these days when sex can kill you."

Another abstinence program which has been sweeping the U.S. as well as many other nations is the movement called True Love Waits. Originally launched at the Tulip Grove Baptist Church in Hermitage, Tennessee and subsequently developed by the Baptist Sunday School Board, this movement is now an international campaign designed to challenge teenagers and college students to remain sexually pure until marriage. Hundreds of thousands of young people have signed pledge cards, which read: **"Believing that true love waits, I make a commitment to God, myself, my family, my friends, my future mate, and my future children to be sexually abstinent from this day until the day I enter a biblical marriage relationship."** Over 27 different Christian denominations and organizations have endorsed and participated in this challenging and exciting program with some churches holding special worship and commitment services in which youth publicly pledge to reserve sexual intercourse for marriage. This touching ceremony sometimes involves the parents standing on both sides of the person making the pledge with the parent giving the youth a ring, which is worn on the right ring finger and serves as a reminder that this commitment has been made. This ring is to be worn until the wedding night at which time it is to be given to the husband or wife. For additional information concerning this, you may call toll-free at: 1-800-LUV-WAIT.

PRACTICAL GUIDELINES

Let us look now at some practical guidelines on the subject of sex.

Word to the Young Men

1. Don't expect to marry a virgin if you're not one yourself.
2. Be responsible. (If men suddenly could get pregnant, much of the premarital sexual activity would stop immediately).
3. Stop trying to see just how far she will let you go with her. You have just as much responsibility to say no as she does.
4. Treat your girlfriend and all other women and girls like you would want your mother, sister, or daughter to be treated.
5. Making friends is for dating; making love is for marriage.
6. Be honest. Don't tell her you love her when you know you don't.
7. Stand up as a strong black man of God. It's not about a condom, but a conversion.

Word to the Young Women

1. Realize that love and sex are not the same.
2. Stop dressing like you just came from Frederick's of Hollywood. Tight form-fitting, low-cut, short, or sheer clothes

SEX MISUSED   67

often send the wrong message, and then you wonder why you get no respect.

3. Don't tease guys. When you say no, make sure you know and they know that you mean no.

4. Respect yourself and make sure that respect is reflected in your speech and in the way you carry yourself. Most guys will in turn respect you.

5. Watch your body language. You can speak volumes with your legs, hips, and chest.

6. Forget about sex just to keep a guy. Sex is often one of the quickest ways to lose him.

7. Cultivate great inner beauty. Recognize the ebony princess inside you, and strive to be all that God has created you to be.

God's Original Intentions for Sex

God's original intentions for sex were threefold:

1. Population (Genesis 1:27–28)
2. Marital unification (Genesis 2:18, 24–25)
3. Marital pleasure (Song of Solomon 7)

When original intentions are misappropriated, disaster often develops. Therefore, if we expect to receive from the sexual experience all that God has designed and intended it to be, we must decide today to do it God's way. These are the days when it must be said: "No wed, no bed! No ring, no thing! No God, no bod! No commitment, no connection!"

Confession and Covenant

You may be saying, "It's too late for me; I've already messed up in the sexual area." Thank God that he stands ready and waiting for you to confess your sins and receive his full forgiveness (1 John 1:9). Part of your confession might also involve eliminating a relationship or not allowing yourself to be in certain vulnerable situations that force you to compromise your obedience to God. Consider the following covenant, and if it seriously reflects the true desire of your heart, sign it.

PERSONAL COVENANT WITH GOD

(Source Unknown)

Lord Jesus, I present my body to you as a living and holy sacrifice. I will not be conformed to the lustful passions of this world, but will be transformed by the renewing of my mind in order to prove what is the good, acceptable, and perfect will of God.

I realize that you want the very best for me, but in order to receive your best, I must abide by your guidelines. Thank you for inventing something as beautiful as sex. Only you could do that, and only you know the right person for me. Forgive me for any sins of my past. Wash me, cleanse me, and make me pure once more.

I hereby promise to stay pure as you give me the power to avoid temptation. I understand that no one is worthy to touch my body except the one you have chosen for me. So I now present my body to you as a living and holy sacrifice until this vow is exchanged for my wedding vow.

Your Child,

_____

Parent Name

_____

RAP SECTION

1. At your school and in your community, what do most of the people think about the rightness or wrongness of premarital sex?
2. In your opinion, is abstinance a realistic option? Why or why not?
3. To which of the four mindsets discussed in this chapter do you belong?
4. True or False: If a guy spends money on a young lady, she at least owes him a little something in return. Why or why not?
5. Should the church encourage the use of birth control for the unmarried? Should schools distribute condoms?
6. Which of the following dating activities would be acceptable to you as positive alternatives to sexual involvement?
    a. Visit a new church together
    b. Go to the zoo together
    c. Have a picnic lunch in the park
    d. Do artwork together
    e. Compose a song or poem together
    f. Create a skit and act it out
    g. Visit a nursing home, children's home or shelter and minister there together
    h. Have a Bible study together
    i. Make ice cream sundaes together or cook a full meal
    j. Look through family photographs together
    k. Visit a library or museum together
    l. Double date with another couple

WORD

1. Read Romans 8:5–13; Romans 6:12–14; and 1 Corinthians 6:12–20 and 10:13.
2. Read 1 Corinthians 6:12–20.

3. Read Galatians 5:16–21. What are the deeds of the flesh and how can these deeds be counteracted?

4. Read Romans 7:14–20. Have you ever experienced what Paul is describing here? Is there any hope for such situations?

5. Read Matthew 5:27–30. Where does the temptation battle usually begin?

6. Read 1 Corinthians 7:7–9. Discuss your personal reactions to these verses.

7. Read Proverbs 31:10–11; 25–30. List several desirable qualities in females.
Read 2 Timothy 2:21–22. List several desirable qualities in males. Discuss both lists; compare and contrast.

8. Read 1 John 1:9. Relate this verse to sexual sin and to what our response should be when convicted by God's Spirit. What is God's response?

9. Read Romans 12:1–2. What must change in us if we are to be transformed?

Role Play

Create the following male/female relationship scenarios:

1. A woman is being pressured to have sex. How does she respond?

2. A man is being pressured to have sex. How does he respond?

3. A group of girls discovers that one of the group is a virgin and begins to tease her. How does she respond? (Repeat this scene with a boy.)

4. You discover that you are pregnant or that you are the father of an expected child. How do you react?

5. Your best friend tells you that he or she has AIDS. How do you respond?

6. Your friend confides that he or she is tempted to have sex but is not sure and wants to know what God says about it. How do you respond?

Special Projects

1. Create a gospel rap that uses the words and principles of God's Word with regard to sex. Perform each rap for your group.
2. Sponsor a TRUE LOVE WAITS campaign at your church which could include weekend seminars on sex, dating, and preparation for marriage. Culminate this with a Sunday worship service in which youth participants display signed TRUE LOVE WAITS cards promising to reserve sex for marriage. Special rings can be ordered, and parents can be included.

For more information on TRUE LOVE WAITS,
call 1-800-LUV-WAIT.

HEALERS

7

FUNCTIONAL FAMILIES

It takes a whole village to raise a child.

Afrikan proverb

In order for something to be functional, it must be operative and capable of performing. It must be designed for, and adapted to, a specific type of use. The black family is a microcosm of the Afrikan-American community. Therefore, when the family is sick or broken, so is the entire community. When the black family is strong and healthy, the whole community thrives.

The family unit must be revered as an institution painstakingly designed by God to model the ideal relationship between the Creator and the creation. Before leaping into a commitment as serious as marriage or parenthood, we must take a look at the requirements for success.

Many see marriage as a carefree ride into a utopian sunset. As Carl Brecheen points out in the book *What Every Family Needs,* "Being in love, staying in love, and growing in love comes from intelligent thought, planning and committed action." Brecheen continues to underscore the importance of marriage through acknowledging that.

It takes patience to grow a marriage, experience to discover the ever-changing needs of another human being, courage to communicate, and wisdom to really know another person, yet, this is what marriage is all about. Those who are unwilling to take the time to nurture a marriage should remain single. But for those who choose to marry, significant investment of time, money, energy, and concern in the relationship is absolutely essential.[1]

A LESSON FROM WILDLIFE

Marriage can provide the means by which we experience the deepest and most profound array of emotions and personal satisfaction possible. Although marriage should not be dreaded or feared, it must be respected and protected. This protection must be enacted against the multitude of ravenous family predators that relentlessly pursue their prey. A wildlife documentary on an educational TV program captured the process of the predatory hunt on film. There were several facets of this hunt:

1. The predators primarily went after the young animals that had not developed mature defensive skills.
2. The young animals encircled by the parents could not be attacked.
3. Animals of any age or size that were sick or lame were also prime targets for attack.

What a lesson we humans could learn for ourselves simply by observing wildlife. As Brecheen points out, only a God-centered family that spends quality and quantity time together can successfully ward off the multitude of would-be family attackers, many of which were mentioned in the first half of this book. Brecheen contends:

Someone must be paying attention, not just drifting along. Someone must take time to investigate the influences being brought to bear on family members. Someone must plan specifically in order that the really good things may happen in the life of the family. We must aggressively take charge like a mother lion with her cubs. We must provide for the needs of our families with that kind of life-risking dedication. We must protect family members from destructive forces with that kind of enthusiasm and commitment.[2]

Susan Bell, director of professional services for Family and Children's Services stated that in functional families "parents set clear boundaries, the parents have certain roles, they oversee the children's welfare, they take good care of themselves, they bring in the money, and there's good communication between the parents and the children." As a youth or young adult, the time to begin learning good parental skills is not six weeks prior to your first child, but right now.

WHERE ARE THE FATHERS?

In 1991, the Associated Press reported that in 1970, one-third of black people lived in families headed by women. By 1990, almost 50% lived in broken homes. So where are all the men? Some are in prison, some are in the street, some are in various kinds of recovery, some are in the military, church, school, or busy with a business. Wherever they are, one place that far too many men are *not* is in the *home*. The father is essential, especially within the black family. The mother and father are the first and primary role models for the child. Words and actions spoken and performed by a parent and especially the father make everlasting impressions upon the children. Haki Madhabuti, in the same book quoted earlier, states:

These days, most black boys learn to be fathers through watching the wind (i.e., spaces reserved for missing fathers). Many of them also receive instruction in fathering from their mothers' discussions about absent "dads." ... If there is anything clear about the Afrikan-American community it is that women are having serious difficulty teaching black boys to be men and, by extension, to be fathers.[3]

A practical aspect of Madhubuti's book is the inclusion of the Afrikan-American Father's Pledge and Madhubuti's Home Rules for children. Below are the rules and an abbreviated version of the pledge:

AFRIKAN-AMERICAN FATHER'S PLEDGE

1. I will work to be the best father I can be.
2. I will openly display love and caring for my wife and children.
3. I will teach by example.
4. I will read to or with my children as often as possible.
5. I will encourage and organize frequent family activities for the home and away from home.
6. I will never be intoxicated or high in the presence of my children or use language unbecoming for an intelligent and serious father.
7. I will be nonviolent in my relationships with my wife and children.
8. I will maintain a home that is culturally in tune with the best of Afrikan-American history, struggle, and future.
9. I will teach my children to be responsible, disciplined, fair, and honest.

10. I will provide my family with an atmosphere of love and security to aid them in their development into sane, loving, productive, spiritual, hard-working, creative Afrikan-Americans who ... help the less-fortunate of this world.

MADHUBUTI'S HOME RULES

1. Don't lie, don't steal, don't cheat.
2. Don't embarrass your family; listen to your parents and other responsible adults.
3. Always do your best and improve on yesterday's work.
4. Learn as much as you can; always expand your knowledge base.
5. Seek quality in all things rather than weakening quantity.
6. Always be creative; do not settle for easy answers or conclusions.
7. Learn from mistakes and always oppose that which is not good.
8. Do homework and housework each day.
9. Avoid alcohol, drugs, and cigarettes.
10. Respect elders.

Certainly all these guidelines, if observed, would revolutionize the Afrikan-American family. We can no longer afford to sit idly by and passively observe the slow and painful death of such a vitally important entity within our community. Positive and realistic role models are needed now.

ROOTS AND WINGS

The botanical equivalents to children and youth are the buds of plants. Without the production and cultivation of buds, there can be no new growth in the plant. Similarly, unless careful cultivation is given to black children and youth, the future will be severely jeopardized.

Most children were born with unlimited potential. Young people can become whomever and whatever they wish if their willpower is strong and they have encouragement from home. Most of America's black leaders did not come from elite families. Environment is not an insurmountable impediment to success. No matter how terrible a domestic situation may be, one should concentrate on the most positive attitude possible.

Once youth have acquired foundational roots, they must acquire aspirational wings. Those who have been further in life and have experienced more, have a responsibility to assist and enlighten those who are younger and are just learning the ropes of life. This concept is based upon the Afrikan cyclical system of passing the torch or baton from one generation to another.

Black youth are starving for positive role models. One need not be a millionaire, movie star, or athletic immortal to provide an example for youth. What is needed is someone to demonstrate how to properly function in the common, ordinary, everyday dimensions of life.

Amid the flaming fireworks of adolescence, as youth are preparing to blast off into the stratosphere of adulthood, the family is the launching pad. Meticulous care and proper preparation must be exercised in this stage to insure a successful flight.

RAP SECTION

1. What are the positive and negative lessons you have personally experienced with regard to black family life?
2. Do you look forward to marriage? Why or why not? What would you do the same or differently from your parents with regard to marriage?
3. Do you look forward to becoming a parent? Why or why not? Would you raise your children differently than your parents?
4. Discuss each item in the Afrikan-American Father's Pledge. Are they realistic and attainable?

5. Discuss each item in Madhubuti's Home Rules. Are they realistic and attainable? Would you subtract or add any?
6. What is the most common conflict in your family?

Role Play

Create a scenario outlining one or two of the conflicts discussed in #6 above. Dramatize two or three possible alternatives for resolving the conflict.

WORD

1. Read Ephesians 6:1–4.
   a. Is there a difference between the words *obey* and *honor?*
   b. Discuss specific ways you could improve in obeying and honoring your parents.
2. Read 1 Corinthians 7.
   a. Do any of the statements in this chapter surprise you?
   b. How do you know if God's will is for you to be married or to forever remain single (Hint: verses 36–38)?

8

SOLID SPIRITUALITY

But seek ye first the kingdom of God and his righteousness, and all things shall be added unto you.

(Matthew 6:33 KJV)

Many of the ailments of society come from today's moral decline and spiritual decay. All of life is directly or indirectly related to God, who is the creator of life. So since God is the source, anything that is disconnected from the source usually tends to decline and eventually dies. The causes for this disconnection point to either conscious or unconscious disobedience to the will and purpose of God.

The Afrikan-American dilemma has been thoroughly observed, studied, surveyed, analyzed, researched, investigated, theorized, categorized, and compartmentalized. But putting a Band-Aid on a cancer will only cover it for a while. However, the root of the problem remains intact, unless black America gets some spiritual help, all the philosophical theories, social programs, government initiatives, and economic recovery programs will be mere Band-Aids covering a much deeper problem. It does not matter the amount of money in the bank if there is a void in the heart. It does not matter the years of education in the mind if there is a vacuum in the spirit. Therapy programs and recovery plans will be of little use if there is still a hole in the soul.

In the colorful words of Reverend Joseph Lowery:

> We have deserted the good spouse of spirituality and we're carrying on an affair with the prostitute of materialism and greed. And when materialism and greed get together, they produce some ugly children.[1]

Since the federal government does not include "obedience to God" as a line item in the national budget, teaching this awesome responsibility falls upon at least three shoulders:

1. the individual
2. the family
3. the church

Let us now consider in detail how obedience to God can be accomplished from these three important vantage points.

OBEDIENCE TO GOD THROUGH THE INDIVIDUAL

A college discipleship group called the Navigators has developed an excellent graphic analogy to explain spiritual growth. They use a wheel with a center hub, an outer rim, and four spokes to represent the life of a Christian. The hub represents Christ as the center of one's life. The rim represents obedience to Christ, and the four spokes represent prayer, Scripture, fellowship, and witnessing. Although many different pieces of spiritual-growth literature contain this same basic growth content, the wheel analogy communicates very effectively. The more spokes that are absent from our wheel the greater the probability of an impending spiritual disaster. Let us examine more closely each of the basic elements in the exciting and dynamic process of spiritual growth.

Christ the Center

The song "Center of My Joy" recorded by Richard Smallwood, captures the essence of this very necessary aspect in spiritual development. God realizes that there are many things in life to distract our attention from the most important elements in life. Therefore, God promises that we will receive the things of life if we will only seek him first (Matthew 6:33). This is God's divine order. His first place status cannot be substituted for third place or even second place if we expect God's precious promises to be fulfilled in our lives. If God's kingdom or rule is not first, then even if we do manage to secure some of the things of life, they will not be ultimately fulfilling until God becomes number one.

Having Jesus Christ as the center of life means that Christ has been welcomed inside as a constant companion (Colossians 1:27). Consequently, wherever you go, Christ goes also. That fact can be a comfort as well as a warning. As long as we the branches stay connected to Christ the vine (John 15:4–5), we will bear much fruit (Galatians 5:22–23). God wants us to present our bodies as literal living sacrifices so that our everyday lives will bring glory to him (Romans 12:1).

Obedience to God

Is it possible to be a son or daughter of your parents without always being obedient to your parents' wishes and instructions? Of course. Likewise, being a child of God does not automatically guarantee obedience to the heavenly Father. James 1:22 encourages us to be doers of the Word and not hearers only. John 15:14 states that obedience is a necessary condition for acceptable friendship with Christ.

One of the hardest-hitting verses in all of the Bible is Luke 6:46. It asks, "Why do you call me 'Lord, Lord', and do not what I tell you?" Just as we cannot be a true student without studying and doing homework, we cannot be true Christians without seeking and obeying the will and commandments of God.

The Word of God

Imagine trying to drive from California to New York without using a road map. Imagine walking through deep woods at night without a light. Imagine trying to feed a baby without milk. Each of the above situations would certainly prove to be very difficult, frustrating, and practically impossible. Similar to these is trying to successfully live the Christian life without the daily nourishment of the Word of God. The Bible may be compared to many things such as a light (Psalm 119:105), a sword (Hebrews 4:12), and a seed (Matthew 13:18–23). More contemporary comparisons could be a textbook, an instruction manual, or even a love letter. Second Timothy 3:16–17 sums it up in acknowledging the Bible's usefulness in teaching and correction. Internalize God's Word, and God will eternalize your life!

Prayer

It has been wisely said: "If you're praying, you're not worrying; and if you're worrying, you're not praying!" Prayer has a depth, value, and worth all of which usually remain untapped by the average person. James 5:16 gives a hint about the power of prayer: "The effectual fervent prayer of a righteous man availeth much." This verse provides tremendous insight for properly understanding prayer. Notice the kind of prayers that avail much: fervent or serious prayers. Furthermore, not only must the prayer be serious but the "pray-er" must also be serious. Righteousness indicates "right-ness" with God. Try talking with God without asking for anything for a change. You will discover that prayer is designed to be a two-way communication between two best friends who love each other. Have you talked with your best friend today?

Evangelism/Ministry

You cannot spell the word *gospel* without first pelling the word *go*. The same is true for *God*. The first challenge Jesus gave his disciples after encountering them on the seashore was to follow him and to go out as fishers of men (Matthew 4:19–20). The last order Jesus gave his disciples was, "Go" (Matthew 28:19–20). This mandate is important because most people meet God through someone else introducing them. Those who have experienced God's love in a personal way have the privilege and responsibility of sharing that love with someone else.

In addition to telling others we're also expected to use our gifts. To everyone God calls, God also gives gifts (1 Corinthians 12). It is the duty of the recipient of the gift to open the gift and to use it. What are your spiritual gifts?

Fellowship

If you spend 80% of your time around ungodly people and 20% of your time around godly persons, which of the two groups do you feel will influence you most? We usually pick up the habits and tendencies of those with whom we spend most of our time.

Fellowship is especially important to new Christians and to those who are still struggling between a desire for worldly things instead of spiritual things. Hebrews 10:25 warns us to "forsake not the assembling of yourselves …" Fellowship should uplift and encourage those within the body of Christ. Just as a fire burns brighter with several logs placed together, when believers band together they are better equipped to avoid temptations, withstand attacks, remain consistent, and emerge victorious.

Some may use the excuse: "I can worship God on my own," or "Those people at church are nothing but hypocrites," but does the presence of hypocrites prevent them from participating in a school's sports teams, interest clubs, or Greek organizations?

Obviously not, or they would never participate in anything. As for solo worship, if God had intended for believers to worship alone, the church would not have been created. As stated in 1 Corinthians 12, the body of Christ is like a human body. Each part is necessary, important, and interdependent. We all need each other.

OBEDIENCE TO GOD THROUGH THE FAMILY

The family unit is an excellent medium through which to practice and demonstrate obedience to God. The husband and father is the spiritual leader and pacesetter of the family. The wife is the partner and helper, and if there are children present, they are to obey their parents as they would the Lord. The family reflects the divine-human relationship when the husband and wife mutually submit to each other, and the children honor and obey their parents.

No family should be without a regularly scheduled family devotional time. If this were done, the current broken home and problem-home rates would be severely reduced. Surely every family that is serious about unity and about pleasing God can take the time to plan vibrant, interesting, informative, and spiritually uplifting devotional times. Try it for one week and see the difference it will make.

OBEDIENCE TO GOD THROUGH THE CHURCH

Since slavery and Reconstruction in America, the black church has always been a natural extension of the black family. Where else could a black man who swept floors and held doors all week finally go to gain the humanly needed respect and esteem generated by serving as head of the deacon board? Where else could a woman called "ole Sarah" all week long by white children whose every diaper she had washed, finally go at the end of the week to be addressed as: "Sister Sarah Jones–president of the Missionary Society"? The only place this could possibly occur was the black church. Even though such scenarios could have happened many years ago, their vestiges are still alive. The black church has always served as a spiritual education and inspiration service, psychiatric clinic, counseling center, talent agency, fashion extravaganza, and social skills tutor for the black community. The church has been *the* outlet, essentially because it has consistently been the major institution within the community—owned and operated by and for black people. Wallace Charles Smith, in his book *The Church in the Life of the Black Family,* observes that the black church has developed as a force within the black community because it filled a real need. He writes:

> The abhorrent conditions faced by blacks in America are continuing to draw the strength and life out of the black family. A cooperative effort between church and family to pool resources and reverse this trend is no longer a luxury. It is a necessity.[2]

Much of success in life will depend on a willingness to pursue the challenge outlined in Proverbs 3:5–6 and make obeying God's will the number one priority. When this is done, everything else in life will fall into place. If we recognize God in everything we do, God promises to direct our path.

RAP SECTION

1. How can you obey God more in everyday life?
2. In which of the areas of spiritual growth do you personally feel the most need? Which is strongest in you? Discuss:
   a. Christ the center
   b. Obedience to Christ
   c. Prayer
   d. Word of God
   e. Evangelism ministry
   f. Fellowship
3. What is your favorite Scripture? Why? Do you memorize Scripture? If not, why not start now?

WORD

1. Read Galatians 2:20. What does it mean to be crucified with Christ?
2. Read John 14:21. According to this verse, how can we show our love to God and know God's will more? Be specific.
3. Read 1 Peter 2:2. How is the Word of God like milk? To what else can the Word be compared?
4. Read Matthew 7:7. Are these the only elements of prayer? What else can be said to God other than requests for help?
5. Read Hebrews 10:24–25. How does meeting together help us to encourage each other?
6. Read Romans 1:16. What can help us to be bold and proud to share Christ with others?

9

EDUCATIONAL EXCELLENCE

A mind is a terrible thing to waste.
United Negro College Fund Slogan

Education is a golden key that unlocks the doorway to new horizons. It is an opportunity to become exposed to the world's collective knowledge and insight from the past and the present. We owe it to ourselves to take advantage of every occasion we have to learn something. It is a privilege to be taught, and we should never abuse that privilege or take it for granted.

NECESSITY OF AN ACCURATE HISTORICAL PERSPECTIVE

Most of the books on world history have been written from the perspective of European men. As a result, much of history often portrays Europeans in a positive light and non-Europeans otherwise. But just because something appears in print or is taught in school does not necessarially mean it is true. Take the Christopher Columbus story, for instance. Every elementary school student is taught that Christopher Columbus "discovered" America. Using the word discovered is very misleading. How could Columbus have discovered a land in which Native Americans had lived for many years prior to the arrival of Columbus in 1492? Columbus only discovered America in the sense that one personally "discovers" Paris when visiting it for the first time. History written exclusively from the Eurocentric perspective is often only "*his*-story" rather than *our* story. But we must avoid throwing the baby out with the bath water. In other words, we should not reject *all* Eurocentric information just because some of it is tilted toward a certain perspective. We must discover the liberating truth that we can learn something from anyone. A child can teach volumes to an adult if that adult is open enough to receive. Try this: When listening to someone speak or when reading someone's writing, adopt the smorgasbord principle. This means taking what you can use, and leaving what you cannot use. In this way your time is not wasted and you can even benefit from a mistake. In fact, mistakes can be a great source for self-improvement.

Two extremely important links that have been left out of history are 1) the rich culture and legacy of the great Afrikan empires; and 2) the significant advancements and contributions of Afrikan-Americans in every arena of life. Curiously, Afrika is referred to as a Third World Continent. Here again, terminology is misleading. This is especially true since many of the earliest indications of civilization itself have been discovered in Afrika. The U.S. educational structure must become equipped to reveal all the wonderful and noteworthy contributions of Afrikan-Americans such as the following:

1. Invention of the traffic signal—Garrett Morgan, a black man (1875-1963)
2. Invention of the lubricating oil cup—Elijah McCoy, a black man (1843-1929)

3. Helped design Washington, D.C.—Benjamin Banneker, a black man (1731-1806)
4. Invented the blood plasma storage bank—Dr. Charles Drew, a black man (1904-1950)
5. Invention of the automatic railroad car coupler—Andrew Jackson Beard, a black man (1849-1921)
6. Development of over 300 different products from the peanut —George Washington Carver, a black man (1860-1943)
7. Codiscovery of the North Pole—Matthew Henson, a black man (1866-1955)
8. First woman to win Olympic gold medals for the U.S.A.— Wilma Rudolph, a black woman (1940-1995)

All these individuals deserve respect and honor for the significance of their contributions. However, inside you is the same potential for greatness that was inside Morgan, McCoy, Banneker, Drew, and Beard. It is God's job to make sure that you are born with greatness in you; it is your job to make sure that you bring that greatness out of you.

VALUE OF A FORMAL EDUCATION

In this information age, black people cannot afford to neglect any opportunity for increasing our knowledge. Let us consider some of the benefits of a formal education:

1. *Personal enhancement*—education helps one become more well-rounded.
2. *Community enhancement*—when learning takes place with one person inside the community, that knowledge tends to also affect others within the community.
3. *Respect*—whether it is right or wrong, this society tends to give greater respect to those who are well educated.
4. *Networking*—when one participates in educated circles, one inevitably comes into contact with influential individuals who are able to assist in the accomplishment of goals.

5. *Personal challenge*—successful completion of an educational degree provides a significant sense of healthy pride, personal accomplishment, and self-actualization.

6. *Financial advantage*—most careers that yield higher incomes also require an advanced educational degree.

Although an education is an admirable accomplishment, most institutions do not easily give out degrees. The avenue toward achievement is filled with a wide variety of obstacles such as discouragement, impatience, shallow vision, and distractions. Potential roadblocks such as these can only be overcome by counteractive positive forces such as the following:

1. *Motivation*—you need a spark to keep you excited about the pursuit of your goal.

2. *Determination*—this is the stubborn insistance that you will never stop until your goal is accomplished.

3. *Setting priorities*—this is putting first things first and realizing that there is a particular time for everything.

4. *Deferred gratification*—this is the willingness to sacrifice present pleasure for future gain.

Why not view each test and each term paper as an individual challenge designed to help you reach your highest potential as a human being? The landscape of learning is littered with the casualties of college life. Please consider the following tips on coping with college:

Concentration – Keep your eyes on the prize.

Organization – Get it together and keep it that way.

Perspiration – A little hard work never hurt anyone.

Inspiration   – No God, no peace; know God, know peace.

Naturalization – Be yourself! God made only one original you.

Graduation   – Remember, that day is on its way.

When it comes to a formal education, you must be persistent and determined to reach your goal. Go as far as you can in the educational process. Coreen Jackson tells the story of how she came from Jamaica to America. At age 16, she was fresh out of high school and possessed $50 and three dresses. She entered William Jewell College in Missouri and earned her bachelor's degree. She went on to Brooklyn College in New York where she earned her master's degree. Finally she began the ultimate challenge at Howard University in Washington, D.C. A few years and many long nights later, she was the proud recipient of a Ph.D. degree. The moral of the story: You can do it if you put your mind to it!

THE VALUE OF A CULTURAL AND PRACTICAL EDUCATION

Most people know that not all education occurs in a classroom. Although a formal education is extremely valuable, it must be balanced by wisdom and common sense. Some people, for instance, are book smart, but culturally deprived. It is an imbalance to know the ABC's of America and not know the XYZ's of Afrika. Still others may be intellectually astute in several academic and cultural areas, yet not know how to apply wisdom in everyday interaction with people.

Take advantage of the many courses offered in the University of Life. Make it a point to travel to new places as often as possible. Travel exposes us to new people, ideas, and ways of life. Adding new words to one's vocabulary can easily increase one's capacity for self-expression. A Chinese proverb says:

> Tell me and I'll forget.
> Show me and I'll remember.
> Involve me and I'll understand.

Get involved … you'll never know just how much you can grow until you immerse yourself in making things happen rather than just watching things happen.

LET YOUR MAJOR REFLECT YOUR MASTER

1. Do well in biology, but don't neglect the Rose of Sharon and the Lily of the Valley.
2. Excel in astronomy, but keep your eye on the bright and morning star.
3. Make A's in science and premed, but don't forget about the doctor who has never lost a patient; there is more medicine in the hem of his garment than in all the drugstores in town.
4. Rise to the top in business and marketing, but stay close to the one who was shrewd enough to pay his taxes from a fish's mouth.
5. Succeed in agriculture and veterinary medicine, but stay close to the one who owns the cattle on a thousand hills. He is the Lamb of God.
6. Do your best in geology, but keep close tabs on the Rock of your Salvation. He's the Stone that the builders rejected.
7. Be a standout in English and journalism, but don't forget about the primary protagonist in the greatest story ever told.
8. Make good grades in prelaw, but don't forget about the lawyer who has never lost a case.
9. Be outstanding in counseling, psychiatry, and psychology, but hold fast to the one who is a heart-fixer and a mind regulator.
10. Study hard in music, but don't lose sight of the only reason why Handel wrote *Messiah*.
11. Lead the class in Aerospace Technology, but remember: "They that wait upon the Lord shall renew their strength; they shall mount up wings as eagles, they shall run, and not be weary; they shall walk, and not faint" (Isaiah 40:31 KJV).

TEN STEPS TO RAISING YOUR G. P. A.

1. Sit at the front of the class.
   a. Helps to deter distractions
   b. Helps you hear the teacher
   c. Helps teacher's image of you
2. Ask questions in class.
   a. The only silly question is the one you failed to ask.
   b. You tend to remember answers to questions you ask in class.
   c. Teachers appreciate input from students.
3. Read over your last lecture notes before each class.
   a. Aids in memory retention
   b. Prepares you for intelligent discussion
4. Ask a friend to quiz you on your exam and to proofread your papers.
   a. Quizzing helps you to remember more.
   b. Proofreading provides an objective opinion.
5. Turn in neat work.
   a. Sloppy work can lower your grade.
   b. Neat work can raise your grade.
6. Study in a place where you won't be disturbed.
   a. Dorm room studying is out.
   b. Choose a low-noise, low-visibility place.
7. Begin studying for exam *at least* three days in advance (preferably one week).
   a. Advance studying allows time for unforeseen difficulties.
   b. You learn less through cramming.
8. Make a monthly, weekly, and daily schedule.
   a. Place each exam date on your calendar as soon as you know it. This helps handle conflicts in activities.
   b. Weekly and daily schedules help tremendously in the organization of time.

9. Take advantage of spare time.
   a. Don't waste time. Periodically reward yourself by doing something you really enjoy.
   b. Don't work for time, make time work for you.
10. Balance your education through getting involved in educational extracurricular activities.
   a. This may mean asking your professor if you can do a special project for extra credit. Don't just strive for the bare minimum.
   b. Participate in leadership positions that may help you in your major area.

RAP SECTION

1. Name the accomplishments of the following Afrikan-Americans:
   a. Thurgood Marshall
   b. Ida B. Wells
   c. Shirley Chisholm
   d. Harriet Tubman
   e. Mae Jemison
2. Test your knowledge on Afrika:
   a. Name at least 5 countries in Afrika.
   b. Name at least 3 languages spoken in Afrika.
3. Share your concept of everyday life in Afrika. Would you like to travel there? Why or why not?
4. Review the counteractive positive forces discussed in this chapter (motivation, determination, setting priorities, or deferred gratification). Which of them do you possess most? Which do you need most?
5. Review the section on coping with college. Which of the coping strategies seem to be of greatest importance to you? Why?

6. Do you know anyone who has only a little formal education yet can give sound advice and direction even to those who possess degrees? Discuss.
7. How has travel helped you to expand your horizons?
8. How many of the ten steps to raising your grade point average are you currently doing? Which one would you like to start doing?

WORD

1. Read Proverbs 4:7. Discuss the differences between wisdom, knowledge, and understanding.
2. Read Psalm 111:10. How can this be the beginning of knowledge? How has a relationship with God helped you in school?
3. Read 1 Corinthians 3:19. If this verse is true, why even go to school? Discuss.
4. Read James 1:5. Discuss practical ways to develop wisdom.

10

ESSENTIAL ESTEEM

If you have no confidence in self, you are twice defeated in the race of life. With confidence, you have won even before you have started.

Marcus Garvey

DEFINITION AND VALUE

Self-esteem is necessary for any well-balanced, well-rounded individual. Self-esteem is defined as "confidence and satisfaction in oneself." Psychologist Abraham Maslow includes self-esteem in his noted hierarchy of human needs. We all need to feel good about ourselves to be the effective individuals God designed.

When you are ashamed of something, that item does not yield its fullest potential. For example, if you are ashamed of your car, you have a tendency not to invite friends to ride with you, so the purpose of the car is unfulfilled. Conversely, if you are proud of your car, your friends will probably get tired of your asking them to ride with you. Thus the purpose of the car is fulfilled.

Likewise, it is only when you feel good about yourself that your purpose is realized and accomplished. Our self-esteem affects many areas in our lives. Even choices such as college, major, career, and mate are made easier when one realizes one's personal, specific, unique, divine design.

EXTREMES OF ESTEEM

We have already mentioned low esteem and the example of one's car. Now, let's use the same example and show how too much of the wrong kind of esteem can also be a problem. Let us say that your esteem for your car was so great that you only allowed a very select group of people ever to ride with you. This is an example not of healthy self-esteem, but of unhealthy egocentrism.

Examples of the two extremes of esteem abound within the Afrikan-American community. On one hand, there are those who believe they are worthless. This is evident in their behavior. On the other hand, there are others who have such inflated self-concept that people can hardly stand to be around them. Ironically, both extremes are often based on insecurity and a need for love.

Consider a typical group of boys in the hood on a summer Saturday afternoon wearing gold chains big enough to hold Hercules. They dress tough, with four rings on each hand, dark shades, and backward baseball caps. Not only do they dress so you can see them, they also ride so you can hear them several blocks before they arrive! Their cars have spoke wheels, bright colors, and sixteen different ornaments. Some of this is just style, but a lot of this is a not-too-subtle way to say, "Hey, look at me! Somebody please pay me some attention!"

Successful development of healthy self-esteem is often hampered by the continuous playing of negative mental tapes, which have been recorded over the years. Such tapes could include a parent's corrosive commentary, an abusive childhood experience, or other crippling events or information. These negative tapes must be counteracted by positive and healthy new tapes. This is a choice that can and must be made by every individual. We all must realize that only when our self-esteem is based on the rock of God's grace can we weather the inner and outer storms of life. This godly view of self-esteem is contrasted with comparing ourselves to our ideal selves, and with comparing ourselves to others. Internal self-esteem, which comes from within, can be elusive. External self-esteem, which comes from others, can be abusive. But eternal self-esteem, which comes from God, can be inclusive. It is everything we need to be fulfilled.

STEPS TOWARD DEVELOPING SELF-ESTEEM

Just because we are born in negative circumstances does not mean that we must remain there. Anyone can overcome negative surroundings through making a conscious decision to change. Below are several practical steps to develop self-esteem.

1. *Discover Who You Are*—Make a written inventory of your strengths and weaknesses. Decide to improve the weak areas and to utilize the strong areas. Learn to be you because there is only one you to be.

2. *Always Give Your Best*—Only through stretching yourself with the challenges of life can you expect to grow. To grow is to move from one level to another. Only through growth can you avoid stagnation. But as you grow, never be satisfied with being just good enough. Compete with yourself. You have been created with the capacity to excel beyond mediocrity. Learn to expect nothing less than the best from yourself and you will find doors opening for you. The world is full of average people who think average thoughts and who do average things in average ways. Why not break the cycle? Do a little more than is expected, and you will see just how quickly you will rise to the top through doing even small things in a big way.

3. *Discover Whose You Are*—You do not belong to yourself, and trying to please a non-owner is futile. Put God first, and the rest will follow:

> Resources
> Esteem
> Satisfaction
> Tranquility

Where God gives vision, God also gives provision.

4. *Never Accept Defeat*—Don't give up so easily. Anything worth having is also worth the working and the waiting. This also means that phrases such as "I can't," "I'm not good enough," or "I'm tired" must be eliminated from our vocabulary. "Death and life are in the power of tongue" (Proverbs 18:21). This means that you can choose to speak hurting words of death or healing words of life.

5. *Encourage Yourself*—Speak words of love to yourself. Look at yourself in the mirror and encourage yourself with phrases such as "I am somebody," "I am a winner," "I can do all things through Christ," "I love myself," or "I am beautiful and special." Our brains are like computers: they duplicate the information they are fed. Develop the habit of thinking big and you will inherit big results.

6. *Set High Goals*—First of all, write your goals. A person with no goals is like a ship on the sea of life being blown about by the winds of circumstance. Your goals should have the following three characteristics:

   a. *Challenging*—each goal should be set high enough to challenge you.

   b. *Realistic*—each goal should be set low enough to be attainable.

c. *Specific*—each goal should be so well-defined that at the end of the year you can easily tell whether or not the goal has been accomplished. (Goals can be short-, medium-, or long-term.)

After setting your goals, you must periodically review them to determine your progress. Once goals have been accomplished, they are then revised or replaced with new ones. If you use them correctly, solid goals can be more valuable than solid gold.

If you practice these six steps every day, you will see a difference in your self-esteem within one week. Like the power used to operate an electric generator, self-esteem can be used to generate very valuable and productive functions , and self-esteem can produce light for the entire community.

NO MEDIOCRITY CONCEPT

*Six Things To Just Say **No** To:*	*Six Things to Just Say **Yes** To:*
1. Disorganization	1. Organization
2. Inconsistency	2. Hard Work
3. Half-Stepping	3. Planning
4. Half-Doing	4. Excellence
5. So-So/Average	5. Above Average
6. Getting By	6. Your Best

RAP SECTION

1. Review the No Mediocrity Concept.
   a. Which of the six things to just say no to do you need most?
   b. Which of the six things to just say yes to do you need most?
2. Discuss the extremes of esteem. On the line graph below, in which area do you feel you fit right now? Is one side better or worse than the other? Why or why not?

Worthlessness   *Healthy Self-Esteem*   *Egocentrism*

0-----50--60--70--80--90--100--90--80--70--60--50-----0

3. In the six steps for developing self-esteem, which step do your friends most need? Why? Can you suggest other steps?
4. Write at least three short-term goals and three medium- to long-term goals you wish to accomplish. Make sure they are challenging, realistic, and specific.

WORD

On the list of Victory Verses, select the passage that builds your esteem and with which you most closely identify, and share why you chose it. Challenge yourself and the group to memorize one of the verses.

Which of the following "Victory Verses" do you relate to most?

VICTORY VERSES

ROMANS 8:27–28

Predominant Principle: All circumstances—even negative ones—can be arranged through God's power in such a way that the outcome will ultimately give God the glory.

1 CORINTHIANS 2:9

Predominant Principle: While we're trying to figure out a good future, God has already worked out our best future.

PHILIPPIANS 4:6–7

Predominant Principle: Don't worry about anything, but pray about everything and God will give you his peace.

1 JOHN 4:4

Predominant Principle: God alone is a majority.

ISAIAH 40:31

Predominant Principle: Waiting on God can be a very refreshing activity.

PHILIPPIANS 4:19

Predominant Principle: God will always take care of the needs of his children.

EPHESIANS 3:20

Predominant Principle: Our finite minds cannot conceive of all that God's great power can achieve.

MATTHEW 7:7

Predominant Principle: If we keep doing our part, God will keep doing his part.

PSALM 27:1

Predominant Principle: When my view of God is clear, I don't have a need to fear.

PHILIPPIANS 4:13

Predominant Principle: My life has no limit when I choose to put God in it.

Does your family have a regular devotional time? (If so, share what you do.)

11

ECONOMIC EMPOWERMENT

Don't work for your money—let your money work for you.

I n chapter 3, we identified the confusion surrounding money as one of the killers of black youth. Now let us take a more detailed look at how useful money can be when handled correctly. The following are short biographies of some prominent black historical figures who have used money successfully. One of the keys to success in life is to use things and to love people. Many people love things and use people. In looking at these Afrikan-American personalities, we will isolate one predominant economic principle that characterizes each person's philosophy.

ECONOMIC ROLE MODELS

John Hope (operative word: *cooperate*). Hope was a professor at Atlanta University who spoke at the fourth Atlanta University Conference in 1898 and issued a challenge for Negroes to escape the wage-earning class and become self-employed. Resolutions adopted by the conference declared that "the mass of Negroes must learn to patronize business enterprises conducted by their own race, even at some slight disadvantage. We must cooperate or we are lost."[1] How interesting that Hope recognized the problem almost 100 years ago and the problem still exists.

Booker T. Washington (1856-1915) (operative words: "Cast down your basket where you are"). Although initially stressing essentially vocational training, Washington, by 1900, had organized the National Negro Business League to encourage more Negroes to enter the business field. He developed a publication entitled *The Negro In Business,* and by 1907 the NNBL had opened 320 branches nationwide.

Marcus Garvey (1887-1940) (operative words: "Up, you mighty race"). Garvey became so frustrated with America's ingrained racism and blatant inequity that in 1919 he organized the Black Star Ship Line to transport black people back to the motherland. But before that, he organized the Universal Negro Improvement Association to promote unity through education, pride, Afrikan development, and worldwide commercial development. This full-blooded Afrikan, who was born in St. Ann's Bay, Jamaica, sold stock in his shipping fleet and developed a chain of cooperative businesses.

Madam C. J. Walker (1867-1919) (operative words: "Cleanliness and business"). Madam Walker was America's first black millionaire businesswoman. Starting from the humble beginnings of washing other people's clothes for $1.50 per day, she invested one day's earnings to experiment with a new hair concoction that would soften and condition Negro hair. She later invented the straightening comb, and her business grew from a door-to-door sales operation to an Indianapolis-based manufacturing plant. Her empire occupied an entire city block and employed over 3,000 people. Walker was also a tremendous philanthropist and contributed thousands of dollars to black social service and civil rights causes in the U.S. and west Afrika.

Martin Luther King Jr. (1929-1968) (operative words: "I have a dream"). This most well known of the black civil rights leaders was thrust into national prominence through an economic initiative in response to injustice. When the Montgomery, Alabama, public transportation system had Rosa Parks jailed for refusing to relinquish her bus seat, King organized forces to hit the system where it hurt most—in the bank book. If they could not be treated as equal-paying customers, they would rather walk. After 381 days of the boycott, King boarded one of the newly desegregated buses and proved that the only language some people understand is that of dollars and cents.

Malcolm X (1925-1965) (operative words: "By any means necessary"). In an article entitled, "Economics: A Major Part of Malcolm's Nationalism," Charles Ross observes that Malcolm believed in self-help through owning and operating businesses and creating jobs within the community. If this happened, there would be no need to beg or boycott. He believed that if blacks were not allowed out of the ghettos, they ought to at least run them. Ross states, "Malcolm X's conservative message included warnings to stop depending on welfare, stay in school, stay away from drugs, keep families intact, and be good examples for the children. His ideas of self-reliance and entrepreneurship are as relevant today as they were ... 30 years ago."[2]

Jesse Jackson (1941-) (operative words: "Keep hope alive"). Perhaps Jesse Jackson's greatest accomplishments have been the tidal waves of inspiration and motivation that he unleashes through his dynamic oratory and his charismatic persona. He has been instrumental in persuading several large corporations to participate in a fair-share program, which involves minorities on significant levels within the company hierarchy such as franchise ownership. Jackson wisely pushes less consumerism and increased production by minorities.

Tony Brown (1933-) (operative words: "Buy Black"). Brown serves as the host of the country's longest-running televised public affairs program, *Tony Brown's Journal*. A dynamic speaker, he

believes that the key to black liberation is economic empowerment. In some ethnic groups such as the Asian community, the
dollar turns over ten times before leaving that community. By
contrast, the dollar averages about only one turnover within the
Afrikan-American community before sprouting wings for other
places. Brown's basic attack is to buy black.

A. L. Jackson, Sr. (operative words: "Self-employment"). While
in high school, he earned money through using his car as a taxi
after school. Following graduation, he opened a service station,
which he later leased to a long-time friend. He went on to estab-
lish a used-car lot and car repair shop, which is now operated by
one of his sons. Perhaps his drive for self-employment is derived
from a boyhood experience in which he worked all day raking
leaves for a white man and at the end of the day received no pay.
Whatever the reason, he has always promoted progress through self-
help. Along with a few other black businessmen in Chattanooga,
Tennessee, he helped to organize and served as chairman of the
Martin Luther King Community Development Cooporation. It
was initially organized to renovate a well-known Afrikan-
American business district in that city.

The cooperative efforts have since given birth to such projects
as the Tennessee Valley Authority Solar Training Institute Site, a
museum called the Bessie Smith Hall, and others. To some, he is
known as Jack, but to this author, he is simply known as Dad.

Through reflecting upon the lives of these role models for
economic empowerment, one can see that a common thread which
runs through each life is that of desire, diligence, and determination. They all knew what they wanted and tirelessly went after it.
Another thread is their unselfish sense of sharing and desire to
help others and give something back to the community.

MONEY – ETHICS = HAVOC
MONEY + ETHICS = NURTURE

Most self-centered success stories are quickly forgotten because the only impact they produce is upon one person's life. But those who work toward helping others are long remembered for their efforts.

WHAT'S YOUR PLAN?

Now that you have been exposed to the examples of the nine persons above, please place your name on the following line:

_____

What will be *your* story? How will you make your life count for something? What will people read about you 20 years from now? Inside you is tremendous potential for greatness, but it is up to you to work it out!

Let's start now: What do you love to do? What do you do well? The best jobs are those in which you get paid for doing something you already love to do! The challenge is to find a need and successfully market it. Perhaps you can use the basic planning formula below:

AGONIZE   ORGANIZE   SUMMARIZE
ANALYZE   MOBILIZE   REVISE

It does not make sense to see blacks patronizing banks, supermarkets, and shopping malls with very little, if any, black ownership in these areas. For years, three debilitating phenomena have plagued black businesses:

1. Lack of capital and/or credit for start up. Even if you have a good business plan, it cannot work without capital.
2. Sub-standard black business practices—What about more courtesy, cleanliness, efficiency, and professionalism? The little things make such a big difference.

3. The myth that the white man's ice is colder. There is a sub-conscious concept still existing in the black community that no matter how good the black-owned product or service, the white man's product or service is still somehow just a little bit better. This myth must be abolished.

Financial instability is often a forerunner of many of the killers in this book, such as crime (robbery), drugs and alcohol (to combat depression), and lack of self-esteem. But change can start with just one person. Ten wise two-letter words are: "If it is to be, it is up to me." You can make a change ... starting here, starting now.

RAP SECTION

1. Name five black businesses within your community. How many of them do you regularly support?
2. Is there an unfilled need for a black business? What kind?
3. To which of the nine role models do you most closely relate? Why?
4. What lessons can you gain from the lives of these nine persons?
5. What are some solutions to the three debilitating phenomena facing black businesses? Are there other problems not listed?

WORD

1. Read Proverbs 31:10–31. What are the economic strategies exercised by the virtuous woman?
2. How can you implement the above strategies and practices in your own life?
3. Read Matthew 25:1–13. What economic principle can you gain from this parable? Who are the modern-day foolish virgins? Wise?
4. Read Matthew 25:14–29. What economic principle can you gain from this parable? Do you think the outcome was fair? Why or why not?

12

POSITIVE PURPOSE

Your life is God's gift to you.
What you do with your life is your gift to God.

I n Lewis Carroll's novel, *Alice In Wonderland,* Alice was walking along the road until she saw a Cheshire cat sitting in a tree. Alice asked, "Which way should I go?" The Cheshire cat responded, "Where are you going?" When Alice admitted that she did not know, the cat's classic comment was, "Then it does not matter which road you take." Even though this exchange occurred in a children's story, it holds a wealth of truth for everyday life. Where are you going?

It is difficult to determine our destinations without understanding our purpose. The word "purpose" points to the reason for the existence of a thing. Everything God created was made for a reason and with a purpose. The purpose of people is to know God and to make God known. Of course, these two functions involve many subsidiary functions. One of the most exciting activities in life is to continually seek God's will and purpose for one's life. Along with this search comes the willingness to obey God's will and to activate God's purpose for your life.

LIFE IS LIKE A PUZZLE

Your life is like a gigantic jigsaw puzzle with hundreds of thousands of pieces. You manage to put together some of the pieces, but you become quite frustrated due to one important missing element: You don't have the original picture. God has the master picture and only until you surrender all the pieces to God will your life be made complete. Some of us try to be clever and hold back some of the pieces. But God makes no compromises and must eventually have *all* the pieces before completing the picture.

NATURAL TALENTS

Everyone is born with natural talents and abilities that stand out more than others. Skills are developed through training, and talents occur naturally. Talents, however, can be sharpened into skills with proper training.

Many people's talents go unused because they have not been discovered or developed. Myles Munroe says that the world's greatest wasteland is the cemetery. This is because in the cemetery lie many wasted talents, dreams, and lives. You were created with a melody inside of you that only you can release. Please don't die with your song still inside of you. Don't die with an unpainted picture, an unwritten poem, an unperformed dance, or an undiscovered cure. You owe it to yourself, to your family, and to the world to take heed to the recruitment theme used by the U.S. Army: "Be all that you can be."

SPIRITUAL GIFTS

Beyond natural talents are spiritual gifts. While we are born with natural talents, spiritual gifts come with being born *again*. Spiritual gifts *always* benefit the church or the body of Christ. If one's gift does not build the body of Christ, it is a counterfeit.

The Scripture identifies spiritual gifts in Romans 12:6–8 and in 1 Corinthians 12:4–30. They include—but are not limited to—the following:

1. prophecy (speaking truth)
2. service (helps)
3. exhortation (encouragement)
4. giving (money, time, talents, etc.)
5. leadership (showing and going the right way)
6. mercy (compassion)
7. teaching (clearly explaining the truth)
8. miracles (extraordinary happenings)
9. healing (physical and emotional wellness)
10. administration (organization of people and resources)
11. ecstatic utterances
12. interpretation of tongues (giving meaning)

Like talents, gifts must also be discovered and developed in order for one to receive the greatest benefit. What a better world this would be if we were all exercising our spiritual gifts. How would you feel if you carefully selected, wrapped, and presented a gift to a person, and two years later you went to visit that person and saw the gift still sitting on the shelf collecting dust? If you would feel bad, just imagine how God feels after going to such great lengths to provide our spiritual gifts, and then we fail to use them. You can discover your gifts through the following steps:

1. *Pray*—ask God to reveal them to you.
2. *Read*—consult the Bible about them.
3. *Counsel*—seek the wisdom of mature Christians.
4. *Recognize*—observe your own personal tendencies.
5. *Survey*—take a written spiritual inventory or test.
6. *Participate*—get involved in service and missions.

TIME

Psychologist Abraham Maslow introduced the concept of self-actualization—fulfilling that dream or destiny that you always imagined yourself accomplishing. Every minute of our lives is full of opportunities to move a little closer toward this self-actualization and divine fulfillment. This is why it is so important not to waste time but to make every second of life count. Time has been called one of our non-renewable resources. The tremendous importance of time was profoundly captured through the poem *God's Minute:*

GOD'S MINUTE
I have only just one minute,
Only sixty seconds in it.
Forced upon me–can't refuse it,
Didn't seek it, didn't choose it.
But it's up to me to use it,
I must suffer if I lose it,
Give account if I abuse it,
Just a tiny little minute,
But eternity is in it.

A contemporary proverb states: "Today is the first day of the rest of your life." How will you spend it? You must concentrate not on the obstacles, but on the opportunities of life. Nothing worthwhile will come easy. Dr. Benjamin Elijah Mays, former president of Morehouse College, once said that the tragedy of life lies not in having failed, but in never having tried. In order to be successful in this current day, you must develop a taste for success like a starving person develops a taste for food, like a person crossing the Sahara Desert develops a taste for water. You must see it, picture it, envision it, touch it, feel it, inhale it, taste it, and immerse yourself in it until, with God's help, you become it.

If you forget everything else, please remember to:

1. Put God first
2. Help others
3. Love yourself
4. Do your best in everything you do

May God bless you; be encouraged, and don't stop until you reach the top.

RAP SECTION

1. If, like Alice in Wonderland, you were asked the question "Where are you going?", what would you say?
2. What is your purpose in life? State it in one complete sentence.
3. Have you given God all the pieces to the puzzle of your life? Which pieces are you holding back?
4. Name some of your natural talents. How are you using them?
5. Name some of your spiritual gifts. How are you using them?
6. What would it take for you to experience self-actualization in a particular area?
7. How could you handle your time better?
8. How has this book affected you?

DRAMA

Read Ecclesiastes 3:1–8, 11. Divide the verses among your group and read alternately in speech choir fashion.

WORD

1. Read Romans 11:29. How does this relate to spiritual gifts and what new perspective does this give?
2. Read Ephesians 5:15–17. Discuss the relationship between wisdom, foolishness, and the spending of one's time.
3. Read Jeremiah 29:11–13. In what ways does this give you hope for your future?
4. Project: Memorize a Scripture of your choice.

NOTES

INTRODUCTION

1. Myles Munroe, *Releasing Your Potential* (Shippensburg: Destiny Image Publishers, 1992), 83.

CHAPTER 2: Drugs and Alcohol Abused

1. "What Would It Take To Get America Off Drugs?" (*Time*, 9 November 1992), 41.
2. *The Tennessean* (Nashville), 14 April 1992, 1A.
3. *The Tennessean*, 7 June 1991.

CHAPTER 4: Homicide Infused

1. "Men, Macho, and Murder," *Essence*, November 1992, 46.
2. *The Tennessean* (Nashville), 24 November 1991, 5D.
3. Judith Re and M. F. Schneider, *A Teenager's Guide To Feeling Confident in Any Social Situation*, (Summit Books, 1991).

CHAPTER 5: Racism Accused

1. *Webster II New Riverside University Dictionary* (Boston: Houghton Mifflin, 1984), 968.
2. Statistical Abstract of the United States 1995, 115th ed. (U.S. Government Printing Office, Washington, D.C., Sept. 1995), 469.
3. Chicago Fed Letter [CHF] ISSN: 0895-0164 July 1995, 1–3.
4. *Black Enterprise*, 6 January 1995, 28.

5. Haki Madhubuti, *Black Men: Obsolete, Single, Dangerous?* (Chicago: Third World Press, 1990), 169.

6. Wendell Dawson, "Love and Respect For Self," Metropolitan Times, 6 December 1992, 5.

7. "White Men on Black Power," *Essence* (November 1992).

8. Jo Petty, *Apples of Gold* (Norwalk: C. R. Gibson Co., 1962), 12.

9. Martin Luther King, Jr., *Ebony* (January 1996).

10. Dawson, 5.

11. Joseph Lowery, Keynote Speech at 12th Annual Nashville Minority Business Opportunity Fair, Nashville, TN.

12. Michael A. Grant, *Beyond Blame* (Nashville: Smithson-Berry Publications, 1994), 42.

CHAPTER 6: Sex Misused

1. Youth at Risk Behavior Survey (Centers for Disease Control, Atlanta, Ga., 1990).

2. *The Tennessean* (Nashville), 4 January 1992, A3.

3. *The Tennessean*, 21 April 1992, D1.

4. *Making Decisions About Sex, Drugs, and Your Health* (Krames Communications), 6–7.

5. Alan N. Schoonmaker, *A Student's Survival Manual* (New York: Harper and Row, 1971), 133–38.

6. The Black Community Crusade and Covenant for Protecting Children (Washington: Children's Defense Fund, 1995), 68 and 101.

7. The Charles Stewart Mott Foundation, 1991.

8. CDC—National AIDS Hotline, PO Box 13827, Research Triangle Park, NC 27709.

CHAPTER 7: Functional Families

1. Carl Brecheen and Paul Faulkner, *What Every Family Needs* (Ft. Worth: Sweet Publishing, 1979), 191.

2. Ibid.

3. Madhubuti, 191.

CHAPTER 8: Solid Spirituality

1. Joseph Lowery, Keynote Speech at 12th Annual Nashville Minority Business Opportunity Fair, Nashville, TN.
2. Wallace Charles Smith, *The Church in the Life of the Black Family* (Valley Forge: Judson Press, 1985), 25.

CHAPTER 11: Economic Empowerment

1. John Hope Franklin, *From Slavery to Freedom* (New York: Alfred A. Knopf, 1974), 295.
2. Charles Ross, "Economics: A Major Part of Malcolm's Nationalism," *Nashville Pride* (Nashville) 4 November 1992, 16.